KYLIE
Story of a Survivor

KYLIE

Story of a Survivor

**VIRGINIA
BLACKBURN**

JOHN BLAKE

Published by John Blake Publishing Ltd,
3 Bramber Court, 2 Bramber Road,
London W14 9PB, England

www.blake.co.uk

First published in hardback in 2007

ISBN-13: 978 1 84454 362 5

British Library Cataloguing-in-Publication Data:

A catalogue record for this book is available from the British Library.

Design by www.envydesign.co.uk

Printed and bound in Great Britain by William Clowes Ltd, Beccles, Suffolk

3 5 7 9 10 8 6 4

Papers used by John Blake Publishing are natural, recyclable products made from
wood grown in sustainable forests. The manufacturing processes conform to the
environmental regulations of the country of origin.

Every attempt has been made to contact the relevant copyright-holders,
but some were unobtainable. We would be grateful if the appropriate
people could contact us.

Contents

Very many thanks to
Jane Clinton, Jane Sherwood and,
above all, to Chris Williams.

Virginia Blackburn was brought up in the USA, Germany and Great Britain. She studied English at Cambridge University and went on to become a highly successful journalist. She was written for a host of newspapers, including the *Express, The Daily Mail, The Telegraph, The Sunday Times* and the *Evening Standard*. She is the author of *Victoria's Secrets, Robbie's Secrets* and *Geri's Secrets* plus *Chris Tarrant: The Biography*. She has also written two novels.

1

A Star Is Born

The year was 1968. It was to be an auspicious year by anyone's standards: students were rioting in Paris, President Lyndon B. Johnson was in the White House and Billie Jean King was hard at work winning the Women's Singles Tournament at Wimbledon. And on the other side of the world in Australia, a housewife called Carol Minogue – a Welsh-born ex-ballerina now married to a chartered accountant called Ron – was giving birth to her first child. That child, a girl, was born on 28 May in the Bethlehem Hospital in Melbourne. Her name was Kylie Ann Minogue.

Kylie was the fulfilment of a dream for Carol, in more ways than one. For a start, she was a much-longed-for child; her parents had been wishing for a baby of their own for some time. On top of that, however, she was also to become the vessel through which her mother's ambitions would flow. Carol, who had emigrated from Maesteg, Wales, with her parents – the Joneses – when she was just a child, had never entirely given up her dreams of stardom. And although since marrying Ron when she was 20 there had been no chance of her ever becoming the prima ballerina she had dreamed of being as a child, she felt that there was still a very good chance her daughter would become a star. A big star, at that. Other members of the family were in the entertainment business: Uncle Noel was a TV cameraman and Aunt Suzette was an actress. So why shouldn't little Kylie go on to become someone big in show business too?

As it happens, Carol had dreams for all her children. Two and a half years after Kylie was born, Danielle, later known as Dannii, came along on 20 October 1971. Brother Brendan had arrived a year earlier, and he was to end up as a cameraman, like Uncle Noel. But it was the girls' future that Carol concentrated on. With her encouragement the two girls learned to dance and play the piano.

It was Dannii who first caught the showbiz bug. She was the one desperate to succeed and force her way into the nation's consciousness (at the time, the nation in question was just Australia; it was a while before anyone was to realise that global domination was a distinct possibility for at least one of the Minogue sisters) while Kylie sat around in the background sewing. Sewing was, and still is, Kylie's favourite hobby; she might have the pick of the world's designers these days, but she's still a dab hand with needle and thread. And back then it was pretty much all she was interested in. 'I was pretty shy at school and I suppose I still am,' Kylie revealed in an interview shortly after becoming famous in *Neighbours*. 'I was a loner – I'd rather sit and sew than run about playing games.' Like most other children, however, she did have daydreams about an illustrious future: 'I dreamed of being a pop star one day,' she says, 'but I never thought it would happen. I was just another kid who liked to think it might.'

Right from the start, though, even despite this lack of

ambition and a preference for sitting around in corners sewing, it was obvious that Kylie had something that other children didn't – something that can best be summed up as charm. These days Kylie is a seasoned professional, someone who has been a star since her mid-teens, but even now she retains an innocence and a fresh-faced charm that wins over just about everyone, even the most hard-bitten show business professionals. And that charm was evident right from the start. 'My mother tells this story about me competing in the under-eights piano competition at the Dandenong Eisteddfod,' she says. 'Apparently I walked on stage, turned and gave a really big smile to the judges, proceeded to play "Run Rabbit Run", gave them another really big smile and promptly walked off – with the prize. I just charmed it out of them!

'I do remember being little and dreaming about the television or singing in to a hairbrush, just desperate to be Olivia Newton-John in those tight, tight pants,' she continues. 'I'd also sing along to The Beatles and the Stones, to one Bonnie Tyler song I absolutely loved and, of course, to *Grease* and *Saturday Night Fever*. I was obsessed with the movie *Grease*. I loved the bit where Olivia transforms herself in to a high-heeled leather-clad rock chick. But I never really had any aspiration to be on TV and it wasn't like anything you hear from some American artists: "When I was three years old I just knew I wanted to be a performer so I started taking lessons." A lot of my career has just been a happy accident. Something my dad said to me sticks ... it's the story of my life: I skip steps one to eight and just do nine and ten, but miraculously I get away with it.'

There was, in fact, a little more preparation to it than she admitted to. Kylie learned her trade from an early age, courtesy, of course, of her mother. Carol was not a particularly pushy showbiz mum compared to the parents of other child stars, but if a chance arose for her daughters, she was determined that they would be ready to take it. From a very early age both girls were learning the skills that would stand them in such good stead in the years to come – and they were also learning the professional attitude to work that both maintain to this day. 'When I was four my mum took me to music classes with a bunch of other raucous four- and five-year-olds,' Kylie recalls. 'I remember making noises with sticks and glockenspiels. My mum wanted to introduce us to different artistic and creative influences, specifically music. I played piano, flute and violin till I was 13, by which time I became a slave to pop music.' And she hasn't really looked back since.

That said, it was Dannii who was by far the more exuberant and lively of the two and it was Dannii who first attracted the attention of a talent scout. The younger of the Minogue girls was in a Melbourne supermarket, aged eight, when she was spotted by an acquaintance of Carol's, who was also a talent scout. On the look-out for a new child star, the friend asked Dannii to audition for the part of Dutch girl Carla in the television soap *The Sullivans*.

Carol was delighted for her daughter. However, in order to avoid Kylie feeling left out, she decided to take her along too. She did so to avoid competition between the girls; in fact, it had totally the opposite effect – at the ages of just ten and eight, the Minogue sisters found themselves competing with one another for the first time. 'Mum thought I'd be jealous and insisted I go along to the audition as well,' recalled Kylie. 'All I remember is that I had to speak in a Dutch accent and I wasn't very good at it.' Fortunately or unfortunately, depending on your point of view, the producers of *The*

Sullivans decided that it was Kylie, not Dannii, who was most suitable for the role. And so it was the elder of the two budding stars who ended up getting the part.

As it happens, Kylie's good fortune also turned out to be Dannii's, as well. Carla didn't last long in the series, as she was soon killed off. She made a comeback, though, when she returned as a 'vision' – by which time Kylie was too old to play the part and so Dannii, who bore a strong resemblance to her older sister at the time, was drafted in. She, too, began a successful television career – one which was, throughout their childhood, to eclipse Kylie's.

By this time, Kylie was attending Camberwell High School in Melbourne. Years later, she recalled wearing a bottle green uniform, which she absolutely hated, and also recalled a campaign by the girls to be allowed to wear green cords instead of skirts in the winter. She also secured a little television work: when she was 11 she took part in a television series called *Skyways*, in which she met one Jason Donovan, who was playing her brother. 'Jason was really chubby, with a bowl haircut, and I was really small, with straight blonde hair and big buck teeth,' Kylie recalled some time later.

There was then a gap in her work, however, until at 16 she got her big break: a part in a children's serial called *The Henderson Kids*, in which she played the part of Charlotte Kernow. At the time Kylie was seen throughout Australia as 'Dannii Minogue's big sister' – in some ways it's a miracle that the two are still on speaking terms – but it was a start and the older Minogue sister very slowly began making a name for herself. Kylie often describes herself, and is described by others, as a bit hippyish, but she has a very determined streak that has always been there, and this was evident from the fact that she used her earnings from the series not to go out and buy lots of clothes as most teenagers would, but to record a demo tape. It was not a great success. 'All I can remember is crying because I was so nervous,' she says today. But she was doing it to broaden her appeal to casting directors: 'The more things you can do, the better,' she says. 'Can you paraglide? Me? Sure. Rollerskate? No problem. Sing? Here's my tape.' It was a talent she was to put to very good use in later years. For now, however, acting was to be her mainstay: *The Henderson Kids* was followed by two further series: *Fame and Misfortune* and *Zoo Family*. And round about the same time, Kylie also hired her first agent. She was on her way.

2

The Only Way is Up

During that break in Kylie's career, it was Dannii who had become the star of the family and it was Dannii who had her own television show, *Young Talent Time*. 'She (Kylie) hadn't done much after *The Sullivans* and *Skyways*,' recalls Alan Hardy, who had worked on both programmes and went on to be the producer of *The Henderson Kids*. 'She had gone back to school and got on with her life. The great irony is that her sister was very well known at the time. Kylie was very conscious of that. She told me it was quite difficult having a famous sister.' It was a problem both girls were to become very familiar with in the years to come.

Kylie was also beginning to grow up as far as boys were concerned and when she was 13, she met her very first boyfriend, David Wood, who is now a hairdresser. 'It was one summer when a whole lot of us used to hang around at the local swimming pool every day,' recalled David, who was four years Kylie's senior. 'All the guys would spend their time jumping off the high dive boards to impress the girls. Kylie used to go there with her best friend Georgina Adamson, but it was Kylie who got all the attention. She was stunning looking, though very shy. All the guys thought she was great. One day we got chatting and soon became friends.'

Nothing happened immediately. But David established the fact that he and Kylie were at the same school and gave chase, with the result that within a year, he and Kylie were in a relationship. 'She always wanted to be famous, always saying "I want to be a star",' remembered David. 'Not in acting, in pop. Or else with her own line in fashion clothes. She was always ace with a sewing machine – she can knock out an outfit in two hours. She wasn't really much of a partygoer. She hated nightclubs – if we went at all it was because I pestered her to go. But she was great fun to be with.'

David also saw the more tempestuous side of Kylie's nature. 'I have seen her cry and get extremely angry,' he revealed. 'She doesn't like to expose her emotions – but yes, she can get mad. We had a few rows over the years. We split up four or five times. Sometimes it would be her that wanted it and sometimes it would be me but we always got back together again. I never had eyes for anyone else while I was with Kylie. I suppose I was like any Jack the Lad young guy at that age – a bit too casual, sometimes. She hated it if I wasn't there to pick her up when I said I would and she would have a go at me. I also stood her up a few times and there were scenes then. But at that age I could get away with that sort of behaviour, just ring her in the morning, apologise and everything would be fine again.'

And even way back then, Kylie was a clean-living girl. 'She didn't like my drinking and smoking at all,' David admitted. 'I wasn't going out and getting drunk all the time but at parties I liked a few. She hardly touched a drop. She is a very light drinker and normally sticks to soft drinks. But she would nag me. And she can't stand smoking, which I like.'

In recent years, Kylie has emphasised how important her career is to her – to the extent that she has often put it before her personal life – and that trait was evident right from the start. When *The Henderson Kids* came along, Kylie put her all in to getting the part, despite feeling very nervous about going for the role. 'She was very shy and insecure,' said Alan Hardy. 'To be honest, I think she probably still is. But she was very sweet. She found acting very hard and it took a long while to win her confidence so that she would trust us and give more of herself. She learned that we weren't there to get her, that we were all on the same side and she could be herself on camera, rather than try too hard or let her shyness get on top of her.' She also revealed another side to her character, however, one that would stand her in good stead for the demanding lifestyle that lay ahead. 'In her audition, she showed that she had this toughness – yet she was so tiny and looked so vulnerable,' recalled Alan. 'She gave a great performance and she had a delightful personality.'

It was Chris Langman who cast her for the part. 'We were looking for someone to play the lead female's best mate,' he said. 'I cast Kylie as Charlotte but the other girl we picked for the lead also happened to be a blonde and we didn't want two blondes in the first and second roles. So we decided to dye Kylie's hair red to make her look a bit different. Kylie was shy and the other actress, Nadine Garner, definitely wasn't, so Kylie took a back seat for a while. She would sit on set between filming and draw pictures of us all, and they were really very good. But I don't think she ever believed how good they were, which was quite typical of her.'

Kylie and Nadine became friendly, to the extent that they used to sing harmonies and duets together, even hoping that one day they might join forces and sing professionally. 'Kylie always had a fantastic voice,' reflected Alan. 'I used to get annoyed when I heard people criticising her voice after she became a singer. There's no doubt that Kylie can sing. There was a song at the time called "I Am The Warrior" and she changed the words for me to make it "I Am The Worrier", because I was always fretting about getting everything done properly. I still have a card somewhere that she sent me. She'd written in it, "Don't worry Al baby."'

Alan also had an early insight in to the way the Minogue family worked together. 'It was a very strong family unit,' he recalled. 'At *The Henderson Kids*, we encouraged the parents to give their children over to us and let us work. It can be quite restrictive having parents on set when kids are trying to act. They need freedom to grow themselves. The Minogues were trusting of Kylie and us to let us get on with things. They were very supportive.'

Kylie wanted to continue with the show for a second season, but her part was written out. She was devastated – but, as so often happens in showbiz, it turned out to be for the best because something much bigger was waiting around the corner. After obtaining her Higher School Certificate, Kylie landed the part that made her an international success: Charlene in *Neighbours*. Initially contracted for just 12 weeks, Kylie was so popular that she stayed with the show for two and a half years. And, almost overnight, Kylie Minogue became a real star.

'I like to think that I made Kylie famous by not casting her in *The Henderson Kids II*,' Alan said. 'It was to be about the lead kids moving from the country to the city to start a new life. Kylie's character didn't move with them, so she didn't feature. I think she was a bit disappointed, but it turned out to be the best thing for her, because she went straight on to land the role of Charlene in *Neighbours*. If she'd been in the second *Henderson Kids* she wouldn't have been able to go for it.'

Truth be told, while *Neighbours* made Kylie, Kylie should be able to claim at least a certain amount of credit for reviving *Neighbours*. The show had actually premiered in 1985 as the brainchild of Reg Watson, who had also been responsible for such gems as *The Young Doctors*, *Sons and Daughters* and *Prisoner (Cell Block H)* when he was head of Drama for the television production company Grundy Organisation I. The idea was a simple one: take three families – the Ramseys, the Robinsons and the Clarkes – put them on the same street – Ramsey Street – and watch them interact. Reg was determined to get it exactly right: according to the *Neighbours* official website, he wrote 20 drafts of the first script before he was satisfied with what he had done.

Now came the search for a location. After a considerable search, a location scout found a cul-de-sac called Pin-Oak Court in the Vermont district of Melbourne. According to the website, the houses were more upmarket than the show's producers had originally wished for, but the location was ideal: it was a quiet, out-of-the-way street near the studios (where indoor scenes would be filmed), which was also accessible via the rear, where large vehicles could be parked out of camera range. The scout checked with the real-life *neighbours* who lived on the street – the Bauers, the Aldingers and the Pierces – and everyone, thinking the programme would be a short-lived phenomenon, agreed to allow the street to be used for the new show.

So, location and script agreed upon, it was time to cast the new series. The producers decided a mix of established actors and newcomers would suit the feel of the programme, and so they picked Alan Dale and Anne Haddy, both well-known faces on Australian television, and Elaine Smith, a newcomer. The first episode was broadcast on 18 March 1985 and was greeted with a waft of indifference from the rest of the world. *Neighbours* was born – and no one cared.

Nor did this indifference show any signs of abating. Producers, writers, actors and directors did their best, but to no avail: they simply could not generate interest in their new programme. Finally, Channel Seven, which broadcast the soap, pulled the plug after just 170 episodes. *Neighbours* was a busted flush.

Except that it wasn't. Most of the people connected with the programme had assumed that that would be it, but they were wrong. Producer Ian Holmes retained faith in his new concoction and got in touch with a different broadcaster, Channel Ten, to offer the show to them. The channel took it on – making *Neighbours* the first show on Australian television to be dumped by one channel and taken up by another – while Grundy decided to tweak its new creation, getting rid of some characters that were not quite right and introducing a couple of younger ones, such as Charlene – originally brought in just for a few weeks as a foil to fellow newcomer Scott. Kylie landed the role of Charlene, while Jason Donovan was cast as Scott.

But still the show didn't take off and, according to the website, it was only then that someone realised what the really fundamental problem was: the programme was set in Melbourne, so viewers in Sydney weren't tuning in. There is great rivalry between the two cities and it was generally felt that Sydney made a point of being indifferent to its upstart sibling, hence the lack of interest in the show. Channel Ten, having recognised the problem, acted fast: it spent AUS$500,000 on promotion, flying a cast member to Sydney every weekend to make personal appearances and sponsoring a 'Neighbour of the Year' competition in which the winner won a colour TV. The ploy worked. Ratings began to climb and the show began to attract interest from abroad – including the UK.

Neighbours was first shown on British television on 27 October 1986, when it was aired by the BBC in the morning and at lunchtime. As in Australia, there was initially only casual interest from the viewing public. When the school holidays began, though, it was a different matter: children and teenagers alike latched on to the new show and did not give up on it when they were sent back to school. Back in term time they watched at lunchtime and even skipped lessons to get their daily quota of soap, until one schoolgirl had a word with her father and suggested *Neighbours* be moved to a new slot in the late afternoon when everyone had come home from school. The schoolgirl in question was Alison Grade, her father was Michael Grade, then the BBC's head of programming and Michael very sensibly took his daughter's advice. The programme was moved to 5.35 p.m., it went on to attract audiences of up to 16 million in its heyday and – in an unrelated move – Alison Grade went on to get a job with Thames Television, Grundy's sister company. In a rare example of universal harmony in the cut-throat world of television, everyone was pleased and no one – as yet, that is – had anything to lose from the move.

David Wood was certainly happy for his girlfriend, who had auditioned successfully for the part of Charlene. 'Getting the part was everything she ever wanted. I was delighted for her,' he recalled in 1989. 'She'd had disappointments before. No one wanted to know when she tried to release a single before *Neighbours* – but she soldiered on.'

It was while working on *Neighbours* that Kylie again encountered her old friend Jason Donovan: in fact, her very first scene had her punching his character, Scott. Charlene herself was very different from Kylie. Lenny, as the character preferred to be known, was a tomboy who left school at the earliest possible opportunity to become an apprentice mechanic. Her normal attire was khaki overalls but that was the full extent of her rebellion – her mum refused to let her live with Scott, and so ultimately, in a prelude to her leaving the series a couple of years later, Charlene married him and moved to Brisbane, where they have now settled down with their son Daniel. In fiction, if not in life, the couple were allowed to live happily ever after.

The wedding, filmed in July 1987, marked a high spot for the show. It attracted record a number of viewers all over the world and intensified speculation that Kylie and Jason were a couple in real life as well as on screen. 'It was a really tiring day,' said Kylie of the now-legendary TV wedding. 'I must have walked up and down that aisle 20 times while we were trying to capture the right mood. I'm sure it made a beautiful scene but for me at the time, I had to think of it as a day's work. It was really weird with the wedding. I'd have people coming up to me thinking I was really getting married. They were so excited and their whole lives seemed to be revolving around it. People look up to you so much and I stop and think: Why? I'm just a normal person and it's quite frightening in a way that they're all watching everything that you do.'

Even before the wedding, though, the show's popularity

had soared sky high, as did that of its diminutive star. At the 1987 Logies, the Australian television equivalent of the Oscars, Kylie was given the award of television's most popular actress. She was 18. 'When it was announced I just went in to shock,' she said at the time. 'I certainly don't remember seeing anyone in the room while I was on stage. Honestly, I didn't think I'd win. I just wish I'd been better prepared. I was so nervous and really excited at the time and I forgot to thank all the people on the show. I am really grateful for what I am doing,' she continued. 'I am really lucky, going from school to a full-time job like this in a show which is so popular. It wasn't until later, when somebody asked me what Logie I'd won and I actually had to say it – Most Popular Actress – that I realised how important it was to me.'

Kylie had gone from being Dannii's Minogue's older sister to an international star in her own right in just a couple of years and she was overwhelmed by her sudden success. Intensive interest in her was building up; for some reason, even back then, Kylie dominated the programme whenever she appeared on screen. People related to her girl-next-door persona and that enormous smile, with the result that she was mobbed wherever she went. And despite her earlier ambitions, Kylie really was taken aback by her immediate triumph as an actress. 'You have to be lucky to go straight from school into a job which makes you famous throughout the world,' she said at the time. 'My face fitted the part and everything took off from there. And although there is a bit of me in Charlene, I don't fight with my folks the way she does.'

If anything, the programme was even more popular in Britain than it was in Australia. Crowds went wild when the stars began to visit London, as the Australian brigade discovered on a visit to Britain's capital to attend the SOS

(Show Organisation for Spastics) awards in 1988. *Neighbours* was voted the best show by the under-16s, while Kylie picked up the award for favourite female personality. *Neighbours* cast member Geoff Payne, who played Clive in the soap, gave voice to the sentiments all the cast were feeling when he said: 'I think we feel more at home here and more welcome than we do in Australia.'

But what exactly was it about this harmless little programme that struck such a chord with people world-wide? Soap operas come and soap operas go, but very few have the lasting power of this innocuous little Australian concoction, let alone its international appeal. Alan Dale, who played Jim Robinson, had one answer: 'We deal with real issues,' he argued. 'If people had to put up with the crap your characters are faced with in British soaps like *EastEnders*, they'd commit suicide.'

Undoubtedly true, but there were more universal issues at play, as well, not least of which was familiarity. 'One of the great appeals of soap operas is that they explore common human situations,' observed social psychologist Dr Maryon Tysoe at the time. 'I'm not talking about *Dallas* and *Dynasty*, which shifted into fantasy. Soaps such as *Coronation Street*, *EastEnders* and *Neighbours* examine possible ways out of familiar situations and methods of dealing with things. Everyone is an amateur psychologist and likes to imagine how they would feel in such circumstances. If you watch something for long enough, you get to know a character's history and become intrigued about what is going to happen.'

Elaine Smith, the Scottish-born actress who played Daphne, had other ideas about why the show had proved so successful, not least of which was the fact that it portrayed a perfection rarely to be found in real life. 'The wonderful thing about *Neighbours* is that it's always sunny,' she argued. 'When people open their fridges they are always full. And people like the fact that you can have an accountant, a mechanic and an executive living in the same street.'

Albert Moran, lecturer in media studies at Griffith University, Brisbane, had yet another theory about the *Neighbours* phenomenon. 'The show's popularity,' he said, 'stems from the fact that it allows us to take a legitimised interest in gossip and in our *neighbours*. Because it is regular, it becomes as satisfying as the news.'

But perhaps the people who came closest to the truth – in their analysis of soaps generally, rather than *Neighbours* specifically – are sociologists Laurie Taylor and Bob Mullan, who identify in their book *Uninvited Guests* something they call the echo effect, meaning that soaps mirror the viewers' own experiences. 'Episodes recall biographical incidents, elicit unspoken fears, desires and memories or allow a more public expression of family emotion than might normally be possible,' argued Taylor. 'A sympathy bond is created with the audience, which is often a family sitting in a room watched by another family sitting in a room. And close-up shots are used far more often making the heads of characters appear life-size.'

Mark Callan, producer and director of *Neighbours* in the early days, adds his own thoughts. 'We try to keep everything as simple as possible and direct it at the ordinary things that occur in every household and in every neighbourhood,' he said in an interview in 1988. 'We are often tempted to use a sensational story but we pull back and say, "That's not likely to happen." We do best when we portray the mundane in an entertaining way.' And the programme's values, he added, are a novelty outside Australia, given that the show contains no smoking, no swearing and only a smidgen of sex. 'It must therefore have some appeal to British audiences, because they are different,' he argued. 'They have a certain novelty.' The show was certainly a contrast to *EastEnders*, which had started in 1986: if anything, *Neighbours* most resembled *Coronation Street*, another soap that – at the time, anyway – displayed a genius for portraying the mundane in an enter-taining way.

With her new-found success, Kylie's life changed enormously. Carol took over the day-to-day running of her life, such as choosing her clothes and looking after her newly famous daughter, but Kylie was now on a treadmill and there was no turning back. 'There's so much pressure on me now to work, work, work,' she confessed in 1988. 'I just can't say no. Sometimes it gets to me. I give so much time and energy to everyone else there's nothing left for me. Every morning I'm woken at 5.30 a.m. and my mum drags me into a cold shower. Then she makes up my food for the day – different bags for breakfast, lunch and dinner. At home my bedroom's a real mess with clothes everywhere – but I know Mum will take care of it. I have a real weakness for clothes and I like her to help me choose them. Mum's really my best friend.' And what of her other friends? 'I'm too tired to chat and I never have time to go out anywhere with them,' admitted the exhausted star.

Finally, the strain took its toll. At the 1988 Logies, Kylie won an unprecedented four awards in one night, including Gold Logie for the Most Popular Television Personality. Jason, meanwhile, was named Most Popular Actor, while *Neighbours* itself won the Most Popular Drama Series category. Instead of celebrating with the others, Kylie rushed back to her hotel room, where she spent the night sobbing hysterically.

By the age of just 20, Kylie had earned enough to buy

herself a £250,000 house in Melbourne, but the poor girl was having a long dark night of the soul, not least because her singing career was also beginning to bloom. 'I work a 12-hour day on *Neighbours* starting at 6.30 a.m. every morning,' she said wearily. 'I'm in the studio until 7.15 p.m. and even when you are not in front of the cameras you have to sit waiting in the dark and smoky dressing room. I really thought I was going to fade away at one point – I lost a stone in five weeks and when I told my doctor how hard I was working, he was horrified. Apart from the hours I was working with *Neighbours*, I had been putting in a lot of work to get my pop career started. I was rushing around so much I didn't have time to eat. In the end I couldn't face sitting down for a proper meal and I was so scared I'd get anorexic. I do envy other people my age. Most 20-year-olds don't have a care in the world. I wonder if it's all worth it.'

Others certainly thought it was: no less a personage than the late Diana, Princess of Wales became a fan. The princess and the showgirl met at a bicentennial concert in Sydney in the late 1980s and Kylie recalls, 'I was desperate to ask Princess Diana if she watched the series, but I didn't dare. I needn't have worried, though – she told me straight away that she loved it. Prince Charles overheard our conversation and said that it sounded so good, he must watch it too!'

There were consolations, though: romance was blossoming behind the scenes as well as on the screen. Jason Donovan had become more than just a friend – although the pair fiercely denied a relationship for years – and Kylie was forced to confess the truth to David. 'I was devastated, shattered,' he said some years after the split. 'We'd never really talked about marriage but I had just always assumed that we would be together forever. I've never totally got over her,' he confessed.

'I've never let myself get so involved again. To this day, despite having met him quite often, I have never been able to bring myself to talk to Jason. I have nothing to say to the man – and never will have. But I'm still very fond of Kylie. She's a lovely girl. She will always have a special place in my heart.'

To the rest of the world, Kylie was being extremely coy where Jason was concerned. 'We work together so much, imagine how awful it would be if we didn't like each other,' she said brightly. 'I have no plans to settle down just yet. I have bought a small place in Melbourne which I hope to live in one day but at the moment I am happy living in my parents' house.'

It was an uncomfortable end to her relation-ship with David. 'I knew something was up when Kylie told me she wanted our romance to end because she had a lot of pressure from work – she was very busy,' he recalled. 'She also said she couldn't trust me as a boyfriend – I wasn't there all the time. Well, that was great coming from her! I had often asked her about Jason. After all they worked closely together and played girlfriend and boyfriend. But Kylie always insisted they were just good friends.'

Kylie had strived for the success she had now attained and was aware that she would have to work hard to maintain it, travelling thousands of miles across Australia just to make a personal appearance. 'I wouldn't want something to slip by, it might ruin my career,' she said. 'Just because thousands of people see me and there are millions of Kylie clones and even Kylie dolls, it doesn't mean I can relax.'

Jason was equally hard working and committed to his career. 'We seem to be working against the clock all the time,' he revealed. 'There's no place for egos in our show. And if anyone doesn't know their lines, they could be out – it's as simple as that.'

Kylie also felt responsible towards her younger fans. 'I feel very responsible because I worry that young girls will identify with the character of Charlene too much. I don't want 17-year-olds leaving home to get married like Charlene did – it would be on my conscience. Charlene is irresponsible and a tomboy, not like me at all.

'I don't have any girlfriends any more because I'm too tired to chat and I never have time to go out and socialise,' she confessed. 'I miss them but I know that if I don't concentrate on my career now, I may never get a second chance. One day I'd like to lead a normal life and not be nagged by people about losing too much weight. Sometimes I do wish I had a nine-to-five job.'

It was not to be. Kylie has never had a nine-to-five job, but then again, she has never really wanted one. She wanted a show business career, and she wanted to be famous. She had seized her chances, both professional and personal, with both hands and when she wasn't working too hard, she was making the most of every opportunity that came her way. And the latest opportunity happened to be a relationship with Jason Donovan.

3

Scott and Charlene

People just like the idea of us being in love.
It neatly compartmentalises us but it's just not true

JASON DONOVAN, 1988

At was one of the worst-kept secrets in the world of Australian show business – but its two main protagonists were determined that it would not leak out elsewhere. Kylie and Jason might have been a couple on screen, but that's where it ended, they insisted. They had known each other since they were both 11, they were just friends and why couldn't the rest of the world just accept that? All well and good, of course, except for one minor cavil: they weren't just friends at all. In the best tradition of show business romance, just as their fictional counterparts had done on screen, the two had fallen in love.

Kylie and Jason wanted to keep it quiet, though, for a number of reasons. For a start, both wished to be able to conduct the relationship away from the harsh glare of publicity. By this time, they were both so famous in Australia and the UK that they could scarcely sneeze without it making the news. Neither of them wanted the intensive speculation as to whether they would marry in real life that was bound to erupt the moment they confirmed they were a couple. And on top of that, the powers that be on *Neighbours* were none too keen on the relationship being made public. Both the programme and its stars had a squeaky clean image – and no one wanted to dent that by revealing the fact that the two had become one. 'If it ever gets out that you're going out together,' snapped Brian Walsh, promotions manager for Channel Ten, 'it would just ruin the show and the popularity of your characters.' Kylie and Jason took those words to heart and stayed schtum.

Kylie's first real love, Jason Sean Donovan, was born on 1 June 1968 to Terrance, an actor, and Sue McIntosh, a newsreader. Unlike Kylie, who had a very stable family background, Jason came from a broken home. His parents parted while he was still very young and from then on he spent most of his time with his father.

Like Kylie, however, Jason started learning his trade while still a toddler, encouraged by his father, just as Kylie had been by her mother. He started taking piano lessons very early on and joined the Australian Choir at the age of five. By the time he was 11 he had taken part in *Skyways*, where he met Kylie: 'The first time I met Kylie Minogue, I thought, what a small person – and she still is!' he recalled as a *Neighbours* star. Soon after that, the young Donovan made appearances in *I Can Jump Puddles* and *Golden Pennies*. Meanwhile, he was at school at Spring Road School in Malvern, where he was brought up, followed by a period at De La Salle, a Catholic high school. He spent much of his youth following his father around film sets, and show business was firmly in the Donovan blood, but Jason actually turned down the role of Danny in *Neighbours* in order to finish school. Shortly afterwards he was offered the part of Scott, and televisual history was made. And very soon after that, the two co-stars had fallen in love.

Kylie was later to dismiss their time together as unimportant, a fling between teenage sweethearts, but the relationship lasted for nearly four years and was initially extremely happy for both of them. The two became a couple in 1986, both happily convinced that the other was 'the one'. But with hindsight, there were already clear differences between them that might have indicated that the relationship was doomed from the start. Yes, they were both blonde, cute, the same age and both starred in *Neighbours* and became singers, but that is where the similarities ended. For a start, Jason did not start taking drugs in the 1990s when he tired of his clean-living image, as is often thought to be the case: rather, he smoked dope regularly even back then. Ironically, given that her next boyfriend was to be Michael Hutchence, Kylie hated his habit and feared that the press would run with the story.

Moreover, although it was Jason who was first cast as a star in *Neighbours*, with Kylie only brought in initially for a few weeks, it was really Kylie who was the ambitious one. Kylie has a tendency to rely on her menfolk for moral support, with the result that she is often seen as less independent than she really is, but behind that frail image, there lurks a soul of steel. She is ambitious, she always has been ambitious and she has always gone all out to get what she wants. The same can not be said of Jason. Would he have ever left Ramsey Street when his fame was at its height? he was once asked. 'Go and live in a caravan by the ocean with the surfboards tied to the roof? Yeah, I'd have loved that,' came the reply. 'I could have been very happy living like that and waiting for the surf. Maybe I will, one day.'

Kylie, who was present at the time, added, 'Yes, that's Jason for you.' But it certainly wasn't Kylie. She wasn't giving up that hard-won success without a struggle and hanging about waiting for the surf was a long way off her agenda. 'Just don't say I look as though I've spent a lot of time outdoors or in the sun,' she said once, 'because I've spent most of the last couple of years in some studio or another.'

She did have time for the odd holiday, however, and one of her breaks led to rumours that Kylie and Jason were even closer off screen than they were on. In 1988, the couple were pictured on holiday in Bali. Kylie was topless. 'Ah ha!' said the world's press. 'So they really are a couple!' Jason immediately went on the defensive. 'Kylie can still be my friend without being my lover,' he argued unconvincingly.

'We went on holidays together because my mates didn't have any time off, but Kylie had the same schedule as me,' Jason continued. 'No offence to Kylie, but if I was to come home and see her every night and be with her 24 hours a day, I couldn't cope for very long. It's not the way I'd like things to turn out and I think Kylie feels the same. It's hard enough working that closely together on screen.'

Their fellow holiday makers were unimpressed by such arguments. 'They were touching and kissing each other all the time,' said one. 'They weren't trying to keep their feelings for each other a secret. They only emerged from their love nest when the sun was shining.'

But still the 'are they, aren't they' speculation continued, despite the fact that the two were by now to all intents and purposes living together in Jason's place in Melbourne. Looking back now, it is almost inevitable that the two stars would have become a couple, given that both were single, because they really did do absolutely everything together as well as holidaying: they filmed *Neighbours*, they opened supermarkets, they did promotional work, they dealt with sudden and unexpected adulation and as Kylie herself said recently, they were the only two people who could know what they were both going through.

They had very little spare time but what there was of it was spent chez Jason, snatching a few rare moments of relaxation; the rest of their lives was a non-stop cycle of work, which was only to intensify as both began singing careers. And still they denied everything – until finally, worn out by the constant denials, Kylie let her secret slip in an interview with *Woman's Own* in September 1988 after she had left *Neighbours*. 'It's quite true,' she said. 'He's my boyfriend and our relationship is very special. But I don't feel it's anyone else's business. I don't see why I have to share everything. I tell everyone I'm still living with Mum and Dad. That's true because I still take my washing home and it's nice to have a decent cooked meal every now and then.'

And so why, asked the magazine, had the couple denied their relationship for so long? 'It's a good thing to have a little mystery in your life – everybody likes a bit of that,' maintained Kylie, who then went on to display rather more guile than usual: 'If everyone knew about Jason and me it would spoil the mystique and there wouldn't be quite the same interest in us.' And how did she feel now that she had left the show? 'I miss being with Jason – that's one of the reasons I don't like going on long tours,' she revealed – before adding that marriage to her erstwhile co-star was indeed a possibility although that could be '10 or 15 years away'. Bad tactics. If you want to marry someone who has not yet proposed, don't admit it – a lesson Kylie has well and truly learned in later years. Kylie, despite her international fame, though, was still young and inexperienced in many of the ways of the world – and so what could be more natural than admitting to a few of her hopes and dreams?

For his part, Jason denied everything. 'It's just not true that we're going out together or that she's my girlfriend. We're good mates and I enjoy her company, but that's as far as it goes,' he declared, somewhat ungallantly. 'I don't want to get in to a big row over this and therefore I won't offend *Woman's Own* and say they're wrong. But the fact is I see Kylie as a best friend and not a lover. I really enjoy her company and miss the fun we used to have together on *Neighbours*. But she just isn't my girlfriend. There's no one in my life right now. For one thing, there just isn't the time. And I know I haven't met the right person. It doesn't make me unusual in any way. A lot of people of my age don't want to settle down at this stage.'

Perhaps, but with the benefit of hindsight, this might have been Jason's major mistake as far as Kylie was concerned. He had publicly denied their love affair after she had admitted it, thereby for the first time raising doubts as far as Kylie was concerned as to whether the relationship was going to last. There was still a year to go before Kylie left Jason for Michael Hutchence but Jason – and Jason alone – had put a real dampener on the proceedings. Many people who have had to keep their relationship a secret crave public recognition from their loved ones, and Kylie was clearly no different from anyone else.

And certainly, at the time, she was devastated. A member of her management staff said, 'She spoke from the heart when she said in Britain that Jason was her boyfriend and she hoped to marry him. Everyone, including Kylie, is stunned by what Jason has said. She is very hurt by it all. As soon as she gets a chance, she'll be talking to him about their future.'

It would seem that she did exactly that. Although Jason still would not publicly acknowledge the relationship, by November 1988, their secret was now widely known – to the extent that they were even admitting to close friends that to all intents and purposes they lived together. Not only that: they were planning a duet, 'Especially For You', which went on to reach number one. 'The single should be out by the end of the year and we're both hoping for a Christmas hit,' said Jason coyly at the time. 'It would be great to come up with a classic like "White Christmas".'

Kylie and Jason had both already started on their singing careers, of which much more in the next chapter, and so it seemed obvious that the perfect couple from *Neighbours* should become the perfect couple as a singing duo. And they were: the song and its accompanying video were as schmaltzy as they come. It largely features Kylie and Jason wandering around separate parts of a city until finally meeting up on stage (very apt for their relationship, some might say) where they finished up singing the song together. Kylie looks as if she's singing her heart out, while Jason looks as if he can barely stop himself from giggling, but the single, if not in the "White Christmas" league, was a huge success, effortlessly reaching the top of the charts.

'Filming the video was no different: we were best friends and we did go out at that time,' said Kylie many years later when it was she, rather than Jason, who was keen to downplay the relationship. 'We were the only two people who could really understand what the other was going through, so it was kind of as if we were childhood sweethearts. There was no difference whether we were on a set [or] opening a supermarket – we did everything together. Making the video was just another day.'

The song, like all of Kylie and Jason's early work, came out under the protective wings of Stock, Aitken and Waterman, despite the fact that none of the three were *Neighbours* watchers. Indeed, when Mike Stock attempted to watch the wedding episode, he couldn't bear to sit the whole thing through. On top of that, it was not the producers or even the couple themselves who wanted to do a record. Their fans had begged the duo to record a duet. 'Lots of kids kept asking when we were going to do it. It was their suggestion,' said Mike Stock in an interview three months after the single was released.

'Then at the end of November when we saw it was the favourite to be the Christmas number one with William Hill, and we hadn't even written one, much less recorded it, it seemed like time to do something,' he continued. 'None of us was terribly keen on the idea because it sounded a bit too much like cashing in, and far too sugary for comfort. So we decided not to do it. Then we were told it had pre-sale orders of 250,000 and began to feel that the market was telling us something. Kylie and Jason had come out of the closet about their relationship, so that wasn't a problem, but they were concerned whether it was the right thing for their careers and wondered if it would be a hit.'

'Can you imagine that?' Pete Waterman interjected. 'It came out and got to number one. The romance between Charlene and Scott in the series and Jason and Kylie off screen was the thing that helped to sell it. There's something very wholesome about both relationships and I think that people like that and enjoy seeing them together.'

With that the interview took off into the realms of fantasy and it is amusing, touching or downright sad to read it in the light of later events. But this is now and that was then. What if the two got married, the producers were asked.

'Fabulous!' said Pete, enthusiastically. 'They'd be all over the front pages of every newspaper in Europe for weeks. That would really do something for the record sales. Then, when they had a baby, that would get them even more publicity and we could do a record with all three of them together! Think of the sales: Jason, Kylie and the baby, it would be marvellous. All publicity is good publicity,' he went on. 'Divorce might be a disaster, but if Jason was cheating on the side, that would cause even more of a sensation. Yes, Kylie and Jason getting married would be very good news. Who knows, maybe they will, soon!'

Jason's singing career, like Kylie's, was taking off and in March 1989 he announced that he, too, was quitting *Neighbours*, an announcement that coincided with the news that his single 'Too Many Broken Hearts' had topped the charts within two weeks of its release. 'For me it's like a new beginning. It was pure coincidence,' said an ecstatic Jason. 'I never planned it to happen on the same day, but it has. I'm not getting out because I'm sick of the show – it's been fantastic doing it. It's just that I feel I've fulfilled that part of me as far as acting is concerned. When you are only 20, there's plenty more out there to do.'

Inevitably, however, a backlash had begun. Negative voices in the music industry were sniping that neither Kylie nor Jason possessed any real talent as singers, and it was only because they had become famous in a soap and were then successfully packaged up and presented to the world that they had achieved so much success. The couple's supporters hit back, and one of them, both career-wise and on a personal basis, was Kylie's younger sister Dannii, who denied that the young actors were packaged into being pop stars. 'Sure you've got to have a good song and video, have the right look and then be marketed properly,' she said. 'But you do have to be talented. Kylie and Jason haven't been packaged. They know what they want and are serious about their careers. Jason is such a nice guy and he's really proved himself and showed he can last. Who would have thought he and Kylie would be so popular?'

And still Jason and Kylie played cat and mouse games with the press. That summer the two were living together in London and yet despite the fact that neither had anything more to do with *Neighbours*, the coyness about the relationship continued. This might, perhaps, have been a sign that ultimately both knew it was doomed to failure, but they seemed happy enough for the time being – when anyone could get them to admit that they were a couple, that is.

One photographer was tipped off about the fact that they were living together in Kensington Gate, a very upmarket area of London, and waited for days before he finally saw the two of them together: 'On the occasion they did leave together, they were very lovey-dovey,' he said. 'They walked hand in hand along the street, seeming not to have a care in the world. Although they had gone to extraordinary lengths to hide their true identities, they could have been any young couple. When I took the pictures, they didn't seem too pleased to see me. But while Jason got a little upset, Kylie took it all in her stride.'

Those extraordinary lengths referred to the fact that Jason and Kylie were deliberately changing their appearance, with Kylie scraping her then curly hairdo back into a ponytail and Jason combing his hair over his forehead; both wore sunglasses and usually left the house separately, with a bodyguard in tow. The local residents were taken aback when they were alerted to the presence of their famous neighbours. 'We hardly see them. I didn't even realise it was Jason Donovan,' commented one.

Finally, the couple really did come clean – again – although Kylie attempted to explain just what had made them so coy for so long. 'Everyone believes we are and I suppose it's quite obvious, but no one can be 100 per cent sure, can they?' she asked. 'If they knew all about us, where we slept, what we did together, wouldn't it spoil the mystery? Also, the fact that everyone wonders about us creates a good deal of interest. If we told everything, it would create a great buzz and then nothing more to say. It would spoil a lot of fun. Just the same, I don't really think it's anyone's business, either. Our relationship is very special and precious to me. Because I have so little time for anything else apart from work, and people are watching me all the time, wanting to know what I eat and what my favourite colour is, what I like and don't like, there's almost nothing left of me that people don't know. So I think it's important to set part of my life aside. That part is Jason.'

And she admitted that it was difficult having to spend so much time apart, now that both were travelling around the world to promote their careers. 'I really miss not being with him,' she said. 'I miss his warmth, sense of humour and I miss not being able to talk to him except by phone. We were friends before anything else and I suppose it's one of the things that makes our relationship special.' And of their joint stage appearances? 'This is not something we'll be doing very often,' Kylie said. 'Jason has his career and I have mine and we both want to keep them separate. Just the same, it's very nice to have the opportunity to spend some time with him.

'I find I do miss Jason and I get quite lonely,' she admitted. 'But for the moment, it's something I have to accept. I do miss out on some things my old friends can enjoy, but then I've also experienced a great deal they'll never have the chance to go through. In spite of what people may think, show business was never the most important thing in my life and it still isn't. Nor do I believe my success will last indefinitely. People will tire of me, so in the meantime I want to enjoy it.'

As for marriage, Kylie seemed to have learned that it was better to play her cards close to her chest, to Jason as well as the rest of the world. 'Well, yes, one day,' she admitted. 'I don't want to do it now because I'd have to face all the problems Charlene and Scott have gone through, which seems to make it so tough having got married so young. I'm not in any kind of hurry.'

Jason was a little more coy. 'A lot of people get us muddled up with Charlene and Scott,' he said, 'and we're really quite different in every way.'

Ironically, given that it was Kylie who was finally to end the relationship, Jason was adopting an increasingly cavalier attitude towards his girlfriend of three years' standing. There were reports that he had been flirting with other women behind Kylie's back. More ironically still, the fact that Jason had followed Kylie and had now also become a pop star made matters still worse. By 1990, the presence of each was required in different parts of the world, making their enforced absences from one another even longer. And still Jason didn't seem to see the danger of such an arrangement. 'Kylie was all for me having a singing career,' he said brightly at the time. But friends of the couple were more cautious. Jason was set to spend much of the year in London, while Kylie divided her time between Australia and the United States.

'It's going to be hard when they are on opposite sides of the world,' warned a friend. 'They are used to being apart for weeks but this will be a real test of their love. Kylie may follow Jason to London but that seems unlikely now. Besides, even if she does, promoting their careers all around the world will keep them apart. They are both very ambitious and getting to the top means almost everything. Kylie will be spending a lot of time in America. That is where Stock, Aitken and Waterman want her to be a big star. They are both attractive. They would have no trouble finding other partners. Jason has already seen other girls behind Kylie's back. I can't see him living like a monk.' In fact, it was Kylie who eventually found another partner first – someone as different from the squeaky-clean Jason Donovan as it was possible to be.

Jason's career has not always run smoothly since then. Now settled in London – like Kylie – he went on to have a string of hits but then made the unwise decision to sue the magazine *The Face*, which falsely alleged that he was gay. Jason won the case but lost an enormous amount of goodwill in the industry and has spent years fighting back since then.

After starring in the beginning of the 1990s in *Joseph and the Amazing Technicolor Dreamcoat,* he has had a lower profile than Kylie, although he is happily living with production assistant Angela Balloch and their two children. Rather poignantly, he gave an interview some years ago in which he confessed, 'I wonder if there is anything more for me.' In 1998, Kylie was asked how she felt about such a comment. 'As a friend of Jason's, as long as he's happy and healthy – I sound like my mother – then that's brilliant. I'm not sure where he wants to go, what his direction is. For every end there's a beginning and it might be the end of one thing, of making pop records or being in *Joseph*, but he has the potential to do so many other things.' Did she feel sorry for him? 'No, I wouldn't feel sorry for him, because that would be negating what I've just said,' she replied. 'I think it's just change. I don't know. I just believe he will find a place where he wants to be.'

As for Jason, he does seem to have a more settled life these days than he did during his difficult patch in the mid-1990s. And of his relationship with Kylie? His verdict is simple. 'She is definitely one of the great love affairs of my life.'

4

She Should Be
So Lucky

As chance would have it, Kylie's childhood ambition
in life was not to be an actress, but a pop star. Now, in
addition to her work on television, she had a burgeoning
singing career, which had come about almost by chance. In
1986 Kylie, along with the rest of the cast from *Neighbours*,
had been asked to sing at an Aussie Rules football club
benefit. She contributed a duet with the Australian actor Jon
Waters: together the two of them warbled a rendition of 'I
Got You Babe'. No one could believe it. This chirpy Aussie
sparrow turned out to have the voice of a fully grown Aussie
songbird: the girl with the tiny frame was pelting out the
number in a manner that wouldn't have been out of place
on Broadway.

As luck would have it Mike Duffy, a producer with
songwriters Stock, Aitken and Waterman, was visiting
Australia and Kylie was asked to go and see him. Intensely
nervous, given that disastrous demo she had recorded a few
years earlier, Kylie none the less plucked up the courage and
went to discuss working on a project together. The result was

her first single, 'The Locomotion', a cover version of the 1962 hit. Everyone was staggered: the tiny little actress had one belter of a voice, to say nothing of a presence that lit up the whole video as she pranced and skipped across it. The song reached number one in her home country and by the end of 1987, was Australia's best-selling single of the year. Carol, Kylie's mother, was as delighted as everyone else, and amazed at the numerous talents her children were now displaying. 'I have no idea where they get their singing from,' she said. 'I can't sing a note. I couldn't even sing in church.'

But by now Kylie really was pushing herself: some reports claim that she was close to a nervous breakdown as she pursued both careers in tandem, taking almost no time at all off to relax. 'I was so sick I had to have a day off,' she explained later. 'It gave me a few minutes to think, What am I doing? What am I doing here? I would rather have a little shop which is what I have always dreamed of and having a little holiday house and getting married and having kids. That would be easy. Why can't I just do that? There was so much pressure by so many different people and I just had to say, "Whoa! Stop!" I had everything but I had nothing.'

The trouble was, of course, that she didn't really just want to have a little shop; she wanted a big, international, successful career. And so Kylie didn't stop for long. After the success of 'The Locomotion', another record was on the cards and this time, on Duffy's recommendation, it was decided that Stock, Aitken and Waterman themselves should be involved. Kylie flew in to London in 1987 to meet the trio. Never having seen *Neighbours* and having entirely forgotten his promise to meet her, Pete Waterman was surprised to receive a call from Mike Stock informing him that there was 'a small Antipodean in reception expecting to do something with us now.' 'She should be so lucky,' retorted Waterman. By all accounts, Stock liked the idea of that, picked up a pen and wrote a song. A superstar was born.

Pete Waterman and Mike Stock remember the initial meeting, in which Kylie looked absolutely nothing like a superstar. 'She looked tired out,' said Pete in 1989. 'I suppose it was like looking at your youngest daughter. There was this quiet, rather shy and slim little girl, who had flown halfway round the world to see us. To be honest, we were rather brusque and off-hand with her.' They certainly didn't see her potential and it was to be some time before they realised quite what a winner they had on their hands.

Kylie had waited several days to see them, though, and, with the determination that has been such a help throughout her career, point blank refused to go away until they had agreed to write her a song. So they did. Mike weaved his magic: 'I Should Be So Lucky' took 20 minutes to write, 30 minutes to record and, as they tell it, they put her in a taxi and sent her back to Australia. 'When she left the studio,' said Mike, 'we honestly thought that we'd never see her again. We could see that she was a good singer, had a quick ear and could pick up songs easily, but that was really about all. We knew nothing about *Neighbours*. We just bashed the song out and sent her on her way.'

The producers were so unimpressed with their new discovery that they didn't even listen to the tape they'd recorded with Kylie until the following week. 'I can remember being at our Christmas party and hearing this record which was so good I went over to ask the disc jockey who it was,' said Pete in an interview a couple of years after that small Antipodean became famous, 'and it turned out to be Kylie. We completely underestimated her popularity.

She's a star. Kylie has the potential to become an enormous celebrity.

'She's a millionairess already, but the sky's the limit for what she could achieve,' he continued. 'She could be the biggest female singer of all time if she wants to. She has a very special talent. She just comes alive the moment she's put in front of a microphone. I've seen her look ill with exhaustion after flying in from Australia, step on stage and be electric. It's the sign of true star quality. She's a very quiet, normal girl but the moment she has to perform, wham! She comes alive. It's really quite dazzling, because when you meet her she's really not very impressive.' What Pete really meant was that Kylie can be very quiet. But like so many stars, she has something like an internal switch: put her in performing mode and she will turn in to a megastar, beloved by camera and audience alike.

There was a very short blip, however: the trio tried and failed to get a record company to take Kylie on board, and so Pete set up his own label, PWL, and released the disc. 'I Should Be So Lucky' was an enormous success, reaching not only the top of the charts in Australia and Britain but also in numerous other countries such as Hong Kong and Finland, previously *Neighbours*-free zones. It sold 700,000 copies and made the 20-year-old Kylie the youngest female artist to have a British number one. And this was just the start. Out of her next 10 singles, she had three number ones, five number twos and two number fours. Her first album, *Kylie*, went on to sell 14 million copies. 'I don't know if any pop star will ever be as popular as Kylie was back then,' reflected Pete Waterman later. 'She just transformed from this innocent non-worldly wise little girl in to a star. She was a tiny, 18-year-old girl, had a huge workload and was exhausted half the time, but as soon as she had to work her whole personality would transform.'

Then came the next question: Kylie was the ultimate in unthreatening girls next door, but would that sell records over longer term? Would she, at some point, have to grow up? Now in her mid-thirties, Kylie still has the body of a 14-year-old, but for many years now that's been combined with a sultry, sexy sophistication, making her one of the world's most desirable women. Back then, though, her idea of sophistication was blowing bubble bath off her nose as she relaxed in the tub (as witnessed in the video for 'I Should Be So Lucky'). What should be done?

Stock, Aitken and Waterman deny they did anything to boost Kylie's popularity by changing her image. 'We never tell any of our artists how they should look or what to wear,' said Pete just before the big change did, indeed, come about. 'We don't change their names, either. The Americans wanted Kylie to change hers, because they couldn't pronounce Minogue. We fought that one hard. We really didn't change her at all. Her appeal is very much as the girl next door. That's the way people see her as Charlene in *Neighbours*, and that's how she is in real life.

'She's not sexy and sensuous. She's not busty and teasing. She's lovable, wholesome and ordinary – she's definitely not a fantasy figure. She's the real thing.' Pete was certainly wrong in part of that assessment – in that Kylie was shortly to become one of the world's most sought-after fantasy figures – but as far as her staying power was concerned, they were absolutely right. Kylie, after a variety of incarnations, is still here.

Back then, Kylie even achieved the previously unthinkable: she toppled Stock, Aitken and Waterman's golden boy, Rick

Astley, off the top slot in the charts and became the jewel in the crown of PWL. 'I think it's a perfect pop song,' said Kylie. 'You can't help singing it even if you hate it and it's certainly gone on to prove that.' Pete, meanwhile, was delighted. 'This girl is a phenomenon – kids relate to Kylie,' he said. 'But it's strange looking back now to January '88. In November '87 Rick Astley was our biggest star and potentially our biggest for the next two years. Kylie Minogue outshone him and that's a real quirk of fate.'

Kylie was delighted with her new-found musical success. She had become a famous soap star and was now a famous singer, quite making up for her early teenage years in the shadows – and yet still the shadow of Dannii lingered on, not least because Dannii had also kept busy, branching out from her own career as a soap star and diversifying into other fields. 'Dannii already had her own clothing range and you could sense that Kylie always felt she had a lot to live up to,' said Pete. 'Some of the more outrageous images that Kylie came up with later in her career were, I think, a result of trying to emulate the wild, rebellious personality of her sister.'

Bodyguard Alf Weaver, now 67, looked after Kylie in the early days for about a year and a half from 1987, when she was with Pete Waterman. 'She was very easy-going and I really liked working with her – I thought she was terrific,' he says now. 'She was very friendly and bubbly and we got on really well. I hadn't heard much of her singing before but I was with her quite a lot in the studios and you could just tell she was a class act – and I've been around a lot of class acts, including Sinatra. As soon as she sang, you could hear the voice. You knew she was something special.'

She was still a little girl from the suburbs of Melbourne, though, and shy with it. 'It was never a hardship for Kylie to do interviews,' says Alf. 'But sometimes she would get nervous about the fans, so we used to get the kids' autograph books, take them to Kylie and she would sign them – but she wouldn't actually come out. She certainly seems a lot more confident now but then I looked after her when she was starting out in her career. I had been to Australia and sometimes we would talk about it – I think she missed home.

'The thing about Kylie was she took it all in her stride – I don't think she was ever really nervous performing. Peter Waterman treated her very well – whatever she wanted he got her. I think they had a very good relationship. It was a bit of a risk for Peter to take her on. He had great judgement to pick her and start her off. There was the odd occasion when she threw tantrums. It was usually to do with the venue. We did do some ropy clubs. She would take one look at the place and say "What is this?" But they insisted, they said "You've got to play these, you've got to work your way up." She wanted to perform in bigger venues – she was very ambitious. I also looked after her sister Dannii for a while – they are very similar – very bubbly and outgoing.'

Of course, not everyone took to Kylie's sugary sweet style: some unkind voices took to calling her 'The Singing Budgie', T-shirts bearing the legend 'I Hate Kylie Minogue' sprang up and a Melbourne radio station took to playing a song entitled 'I Should Be So Yucky'. Matters got worse still when Daniel Abineri, a British-born singer and actor, released another spoof, this one entitled 'I Can See Your Nipples', a reference to Kylie's holiday in Bali with Jason. This proved to be an insult too far. 'This is a cheap, crude attempt to cash in on Kylie's name,' snapped a very irritated spokesman for the star. 'We'll pull out all the stops to have the disc banned.' Abineri himself retorted, 'I don't know what all the fuss is about. It's just a fun send-up of a very popular young lady. Kylie obviously hasn't a sense of humour.'

These days Kylie has a very good sense of humour: she is as self-deprecating as anyone involved in the music business and well understands that her success owes as much to luck as to talent. Back then, though, for all her international standing, and despite the fact that she'd been a couple with Jason for some years, she was in many ways little more than a child and all the teasing – not all of it meant that kindly – was having an adverse effect on her. Noticing this, Kylie's friends were beginning to develop a sense of humour bypass too.

'Leave her alone,' snapped Kylie's fellow *Neighbours* star Anne Charleston, who played Madge Bishop in the soap. 'Kylie has been very upset by some of the criticism, although she is now a lot more confident than she was. But the whole cast was very angry about what was being done to her. We are a very close company and all like each other. But it was Kylie they went for in particular. Kylie is now coping a lot better with all this. I wouldn't say Kylie is tough, but she is not stupid and now knows not to take things to heart.'

But they didn't leave her alone; indeed, Jason started coming in for some flak, too. At the beginning of 1989, by the time both had left *Neighbours* to carve out solo singing careers, they were sneered at by *The Bulletin*, a mass circulation magazine, which did an annual round up of famous Australians. Kylie was 'a poor little thing' and Jason a 'flaxen haired warbler.' 'Jason teamed up with former co-star Kylie Minogue to make a flop record "Everything For You"' it sneered – though someone subsequently pointed out that it had actually been called 'Especially For You' and that far from being a flop it had reached number one in Britain and sold one million copies worldwide.

The jibes were becoming increasingly unfair and Dannii stepped in to defend her sister. 'She [Kylie] has had to toughen up just to survive,' Dannii commented. 'She has changed from being an innocent into someone who can cope with show business at its worst. It has forced her to lose some of her innocence, but how else do you get through in this business? Kylie has cried over the things that have been said about her in Australia. She has done so much but Britain seems to respect her much more.

'It's terrible for Kylie. There are radio stations here that refuse to play her records. It's such an insult. They claim her records are naff. Yet every time there is a pop poll, Kylie comes out on top. The other night she won an Aria Award in Sydney. It was a great achievement, yet people were scathing. She felt elated and downcast at the same time. I keep telling Kylie it doesn't matter. "Look at Michael Jackson," I tell her. "He has had more things said about him than anyone and he's the greatest star in the world." If folk want to be bitchy, then let them. The real proof of Kylie's ability is that people like her music and keep watching her on TV.'

It was a very supportive move on Dannii's part and indeed, throughout their lives, when one Minogue sister has been up against it, the other has come to her support. And yet, beneath the surface, the old rivalry with Dannii still bubbled. 'Kylie idolised Dannii and no matter how big she became she always thought Dannii would be bigger,' says Pete Waterman. 'We were offered the chance to sign Dannii but there was no way we could do it. It would have dented Kylie's confidence. And anyway, Dannii's not an artist. She's someone who's good at getting publicity.'

Someone the team were prepared to sign, however, was Kylie's old chum Jason Donovan – actually then still her boyfriend – whom some people suspected of being slightly jealous of Kylie's success. He followed Kylie to the UK to talk to the producers, although he remained outwardly cautious. 'We're talking about it, we'll just have to wait and see,' he said in an interview before his debut on Terry Wogan's talk show.

'It's on the cards and hopefully it will all come together in a week or so.' And were he and Kylie actually more than just good friends? asked an interviewer, given that the two had resumed their cat-and-mouse game with the press. 'I have known Kylie since she was 13 and I can't see why people can't understand why we can still be friends and not have a relationship,' Jason snapped. 'I haven't got a girlfriend, I'm a free body and I would certainly think twice about marriage. But I'm only 19, I've got a lot of things to do and I don't really want to be tied down.'

Kylie felt the same way – she had by now quit *Neighbours* for pastures new, and Jason shortly afterwards followed suit, but she vehemently denied suggestions that she thought she'd got too big for the show. 'It really hurt that people thought that,' she said. 'They think I'm made of steel but I'm not.' In fact, Kylie was well aware of how fortunate she'd been. 'I owe a hell of a lot to *Neighbours* and I will always remember that,' she said at a later date. 'Okay, so it isn't *Gone With The Wind*, but it's popular, very popular, and I'm proud to have been associated with it.'

On another occasion, however, a different version of the truth seemed to emerge. It suggested that Kylie had always seen *Neighbours* as nothing more than a stepping stone to higher things. 'Naturally I welcomed the opportunity of appearing in it, because it opened the show business door to me,' she said in an unguarded moment. 'But I couldn't wait to get out of it as soon as possible. I never liked soaps, whether they're home produced or imported. To be honest, and in spite of its success, *Neighbours* is rough. I mean, if you analyse it, it's the story of three families and everything happens to them. It's all rather implausible and sometimes I have to grit my teeth when I film an unlikely situation. I shudder at the speed it's turned out day after day. The writers are usually still working on the script when we've started filming.' Suddenly she collected herself. 'Of course, I'm not complaining,' she added hastily. '*Neighbours* has been marvellous for me. I'm just amazed that so many people are addicted to it. Trouble is that it gives a completely distorted view of normal life in Australia.' In fact, Kylie was already ready to leave Oz. 'I want to operate out of London because that's where it's all happening,' she revealed.

Not all her *Neighbours* co-stars were as supportive as Anne Charleston had been, though, especially when Kylie appeared to be letting her fabulous success go to her head. In November 1988 she was in Britain for the Royal Variety Command Show, as was the rest of the cast of *Neighbours*. Kylie, who by now also had a successful singing career, refused to allow herself to be photographed with them. 'I just don't know what's got in to her,' spat an unnamed *Neighbours* star. 'She's got her own life now,' said her erstwhile co-star Stefan Dennis. 'I suppose that's it as far as we're concerned.' They were bitter words – but the truth of the matter was that Kylie really was about to leave all her old co-stars behind.

It would take a while for that new life to be sorted out. As it happens, her next starring role was to be in a much-derided film entitled *The Delinquents*. But before she started work on that film, in an odd foreshadowing of what was to come, Kylie was talking excitedly about appearing in a TV film set in the 1950s, in which she would play a priest's mistress. 'It's a long way from *Neighbours*, but it sounds like good fun,' she gushed. 'It's a Fifties love story and looks steamier than it is. I'm not going to do any sex scenes.' Intriguingly, when Kylie was asked who she would like to take on the role of the priest, she named two people. 'I would be thrilled to make love to either of them … on screen,' she confessed impishly. 'They are my heroes.' Mel Gibson was one – hardly a surprising choice given that Mel was and is a leading Australian heart-throb. The other name was one that was known not for acting, but for music: Michael Hutchence.

First, however, it was time for one of Kylie's more misjudged adventures: a starring role as 15-year-old Lola in the £10-million film *The Delinquents*. Set in 1950s Australia, the film tells the story of a young couple who battle to be together against all the odds: separation, abortions, passionate love scenes, drugs, drink, a fate involving working in a launderette and a topless Kylie all combined to shock a few delicate souls and launch Kylie into a career as a sex bomb. She had made it as a television star and a singer, so why not as a film star too?

No reason at all really, except for one: the film was absolutely terrible. For some reason, all of Kylie's movies, with the one exception of *Moulin Rouge*, have been best forgotten and this one really is no exception. You can sometimes tell when a film is going to be a real turkey right from the outset – something that is certainly the case here. A very early warning signal should be that the teenagers' disaffection would appear to stem from not being able to get in to the cinema, not because they were disruptive influences, but because the auditorium was full. There may be less plausible reasons to take against society, but it's hard to think of one off-hand.

There were other early hints that the film might not live up to expectations. First David Bowie, who was supposed to have been writing the music for the film, pulled out because he hated the script. Then Pete Waterman, no less, refused to be involved, because the film-makers wanted him to remix a string of 1950s rock 'n' roll originals, as opposed to writing original music for the film. 'They basically wanted rehashed oldies and I don't see the point,' he commented, tersely – though after a plea from Kylie, he did help her out with one song: 'Tears On My Pillow', which gave her another hit single.

Whatever its shortcomings, this was Kylie's film debut, and one clearly influenced by her heroine Olivia Newton-John. Like Olivia in *Grease*, Kylie was transformed in the course of the film from sweet girl to pouting sex bomb, but that's pretty much where the resemblance between the two films ends. With hindsight, that might have been to Kylie's advantage, given that her staying power has quite matched that of her idol, but at the time everyone, but everyone, saw her as the next ONJ. 'Hollywood is her ultimate professional goal,' explained a friend. 'She has been compared to Olivia Newton-John because she is Australian and because she combines singing and acting. Olivia is certainly one of her idols. Kylie would love to do what she has done.'

Kylie was certainly in one of her more driven modes. At her twenty-first birthday party, she surprised her family and her friends when she made an emotional speech apologising for not being able to spend more time with them and promising to do so in the future. She also confessed to lingering doubts regarding her star status. 'I can't be too comfortable with where I am because I could be a nobody tomorrow,' she confessed. 'The demands never end. You really are giving away a part of yourself. When I am tired and think I don't want to do this anymore, I just tell myself that I might not be here in a few months and that there are millions who would kill to be where I am. It's lonely at the top sometimes. There are so many people who want me to do things and I feel I can't let them down.'

To be honest, not everyone realised she was at the top. Charlie Schlatter, Kylie's American-born co-star in the film, remembers when he was first told the identity of his partner in crime. 'I didn't know who she was,' he admitted. 'I had no idea how big she was in Britain and Australia until the film company told me and said they thought she would be a good actress.' He learned pretty quickly who Kylie was, though: over in Australia Charlie was just a little-known Yank actor lucky enough to be cast alongside the nation's sweetheart.

Neither was their first meeting particularly auspicious. Charlie had just got off an 18-hour flight from the United States and was in no fit state to meet anyone. 'I said, "I'm sorry I can't even focus on your face, I've got terrible jet lag," Charlie recalled. 'But the next day we read the script and we had a really nice friendship. When I first saw her I was glad she was shorter than I am [Charlie is 5'7"]. I thought, I am going to look good. She is very normal, very down to earth. She didn't go on about what she was doing. I didn't know if it helped that I didn't know who she was, but it certainly didn't hurt, either.'

Kylie quickly endeared herself to everyone on the film with her freshness and generosity: aware that many people would be expecting Kylie the diva, she was at pains to assure them that she was really part of the crew. She also paid for an impromptu birthday party for Charlie at the end of the first day of filming, a very wise act indeed on her part that made her popular with everyone. 'Kylie was very generous, very much the leading lady, which was very impressive,' said Todd Boyce, who also played a part in the film.

There was the inevitable speculation about an off-screen romance, not least because the two stars of the film were seen taking bicycle rides together (in fact, they were rehearsing scenes in the film) but in this case the rumours really would seem to be completely unfounded. 'Charlie's a great mate, but that's just about it, I'm afraid,' said Kylie. It was, however, a first experience for both in that neither had done explicit on screen love scenes before. 'It was not as erotic filming a love scene as some people think,' revealed Charlie. 'It was a lot tougher than I thought it would be. It was the first time I had done love scenes on screen, which was one of the reasons I chose to do the film.

'I have never played a romantic character before. I think it helped that it was the first time Kylie had done a scene like that, too. There was a lot of raw energy there, which was good because some things took a lot of takes. But she was really professional about it. There was one nude scene, though I had to do it on my own and it was a closed set because they don't want to make you feel uncomfortable. But when I looked up, all the crew there were women. It was very funny. The crew were great, they were real ladies and gentlemen.'

By this time, as news filtered out that Australia's sweetheart was to be filming some truly shocking scenes compared to her previous work on television, the film was beginning to provoke a tide of moral outrage. Charlie was scathing. 'I really feel bad for those people if their lives are so sheltered and all they have to complain about is this,' he raged. 'I am 23. I want to do projects that are fun or say something socially or spiritually. Sexy is such a tough word to define. To me a woman with thick wool socks can be sexy. It is not a sexual movie. It is not pornography. There is one love scene in it, the first time they make love, when their characters are very uncomfortable. I think some people might experience that discomfort again, recalling the time they lost their virginity. I think it is fine to make someone feel like that, to put them in touch with that feeling.'

It seems incredible now that anyone was so shocked by the film, but many people were genuinely taken aback that their favourite TV star was showing an altogether less wholesome side. One commercial for the film was banned on British television because, according to the IBA and ITV Association, it 'contained material that was too near the knuckle'. (The clip in question had Kylie gazing at Charlie and saying, 'Make love to me,' followed by the comment, 'I love the way he looks when he's just about to …')

Kylie herself reacted angrily to the ban and defended her character. 'Lola is very powerful and very sensitive and she goes through a lot of changes,' she insisted. 'I felt there was something there I could grab hold of, whereas a lot of the scripts that were offered to me before were pretty crummy. There were a lot of seductive scenes and that sort of stuff and a lot of the characters that were a complete copy of Charlene and I wanted to get away from that.'

And then there was Kylie's ambition. With every success she's had in her life – and with every failure, too – Kylie's ambition has grown and now, with her first film on the go, her desire to succeed was more intense than ever. 'I always think there's more to do,' she said. 'And I've got so much more to learn. This is my first film. I've never done theatre; I've never done songwriting; I haven't done much live work. There's a multitude of things to do. I'm interested in things outside of entertainment as well, and although I feel older than 21, I have to remind myself that I am 21 and I've got a lot of years ahead.

'This was my big one, my debut. You can't do a debut again, can you? You only get one chance at it. I think I was a little bit nervous because there are so many expectations of me. But I'd just like to do a good job for myself.'

Kylie admitted, however, that it was a big change for her image to go from sweet little Charlene to raunchy ol' Lola. 'When I think everyone's going to see it, it makes me blush,' she admitted happily. 'But I still feel I've done the right thing. You don't see me completely nude. And at least I feel like I've grown up. I don't think I'll lose any fans. I may gain wider acceptance.'

And then the film opened. For an all-too-brief spell, it looked as if *The Delinquents* might actually do well. It took about £1 million in its first few days and looked as if it might even overshadow *Batman*, which had also just come out. A Warner Brothers spokeswoman declared, 'We don't have exact figures but *The Delinquents* has had a huge opening. It's not as good as Batman yet, but it's definitely up there.'

And then reality hit. One review (one of the kinder reviews, at that) put the film straight into the top ten worst movies of 1989. 'Poor old Kylie,' it said. 'She loses her virginity at 15 to a teenage rebel. Her mother drags her off the train taking the couple to a new life and forces pregnant Kylie to have an abortion. And that's just for starters! I imagine we're supposed to take this load of old Australian codswallop seriously. But you would need a heart of stone not to laugh helplessly at the ludicrous plot and awful acting. Kylie's fans will probably love every awful minute. Others should avoid it like the plague.'

Most critics were harsher still. 'Images stick in the gullet,' snapped one. 'The 15-year-old Kylie character Lola (cliché *Lolita* connotations here) being driven to the abortion clinic by her evil and selfish mother; Lola staggering out after the abortion, barely able to walk; sheet tossing sex scenes every five minutes (or so it seems) after boy meets girl; bare breasts and buttocks; sex, sex and more sex, with Kylie's crackling and cockatoo whooping.' And from another: 'Pulp fiction manipulated by an army of fat cats counting shekels behind the myth that is Minogue.' And another: 'Ultimately, *The Delinquents* is a weakly handled, insubstantial film. Kylie has as much acting charisma as cold porridge.'

Poor Kylie. It wasn't what she had expected at all and although the film briefly topped the charts in Britain and got to number three in Australia, it flopped in the United States and is now remembered as a severe embarrassment for all concerned. More recently, nude shots were published in the newspapers that were actually stills from the film of Kylie lying naked on a bed. The star did not take this reminder of her past very well; she was absolutely furious. 'The last thing Kylie needs is someone digging out old pictures to ruin things for her,' a friend told the press.

The pictures ruined nothing (these days the great viewing public is far more interested in the mature Kylie's bottom than the ingénue Kylie's nakedness) but they certainly reminded Kylie of a film she would really rather forget. And even back then, as the reception to *The Delinquents* became increasingly hostile, she quickly started sounding more resigned as to whether her fans would like the film or not. She also hastily started talking about her next project – a second album called *Enjoy Yourself* with Stock, Aitken and Waterman. As a matter of fact, all things considered, Kylie was appearing remarkably upbeat for a woman whose cinematic debut had been so well and truly panned. At first, onlookers put it down to the resumption of her musical career. But her latest collaboration with her mentors was not the only thing putting a spring in Kylie's step – something, or rather, someone – was providing a distraction from the dismal reviews, too. Kylie's relationship with Jason was – unbeknownst to the latter – finally at an end. She had met another man.

5

Corrupting
Kylie Minogue

It was a beautiful day to be flying across Australia. The sun beat down from the cloudless azure sky; far below, the dramatic landscape of that great country stretched as far as the eye could see. Bob Hawke, the Australian prime minister, stretched out in his chair and relaxed. Suddenly, behind him, he heard a giggle. Then another one. And then another. Bob turned round.

The first-class cabin of the Qantas airliner was nearly empty, but two rows behind him, he spotted a couple who appeared to be sitting in one seat. Both looked vaguely familiar and just as Bob was about to turn back, the male half of the couple happened to look up and catch his eye – and it was at that moment that Bob suddenly realised what was going on. He gave a quick wink and settled back in his seat. Bob Hawke, the Australian prime minister, had just caught Michael Hutchence and Kylie Minogue apparently having sex on a plane.

'Not in the toilet,' insisted Nick Egan, a great friend of Michael's, who was clearly keen to clarify the situation when news of the incident got out. 'On the seat just behind him. She was so small he just put a blanket over her. Two rows ahead was Bob Hawke who happened to look round and catch a look back – and gave them a wink in the middle of the act. That's perhaps the sort of thing Kylie wouldn't have done a couple of years beforehand …'

You can say that again. By then, Kylie and Michael were nearly a year into the relationship that had changed her life and still no one could believe it: Kylie Minogue and Michael *Hutchence?* Michael Hutchence and Kylie *Minogue?* But the rumours were true: the most unlikely couple in show business were indeed together and both were revelling in it. When asked what he was up to with Kylie, Michael replied with a chuckle, 'I'm just corrupting her at the moment – it's my hobby. Or perhaps she's corrupting me, I dunno, it works both ways.'

It was an unusual pairing, by anyone's standards. Up until now, there had been only two romantic interests in Kylie's life: her first boyfriend David Wood and her squeaky-clean co-star Jason Donovan. But now rock's baddest boy and soap's sweetest star were being spoken of as an item and the world was agog. So what on earth was it that made Michael fall in love with her? She was a very sweet girl, but 'girl' was the key word. Look at pictures and videos of her back then and what stands out, apart from the 1980s clothes and hairstyles, is naivety. If this was a girl who had seen the dark side of life, then Michael Hutchence was Mahatma Gandhi. Just what did he see in her?

'I don't know,' said Kylie, when asked the same question in an interview a few years ago. 'But at the time we started dating I was, you know – pull out a picture of me at that time and you'd be going, "Yuk!" And he told me a story about being somewhere and I think maybe I came on the television or something and different people in the room said … something nasty about me, and Michael said, "I like her. I think she's good." This was before we'd met and I just remember that story sticking to me.' Did he fancy her? 'Yes. I really don't know why. I can't figure that one out but, um, yes. He did.' Actually, that one is not so hard to figure out. Kylie had almost exactly the same figure then as she does now – she just dresses it differently. Michael Hutchence was clearly a man ahead of his time.

There are various stories about how the couple met, the most colourful being that in 1988 Michael approached Kylie in Benny's bar in King's Cross, the red light district of Sydney, uttering the immortal line, 'I don't know what we should do first – have lunch or have sex.' Another version has it that he ran over to her screaming, 'I want to fuck you! I want to fuck you!'

As Kylie recalls the occasion, the first story is true. 'I was so young, about 19 or 20, and I remember being overly protected by some bodyguards, who must have thought I was too innocent to be in a place like that,' she says. 'I felt crowded, pushed into a corner. Anyway, Michael Hutchence sort of stumbled by – he was probably really drunk – and I think his first ever words to me were: "I don't know what we should do first, have lunch or have sex." That was entirely shocking to me … then.' Funnily enough, Jason Donovan, who was present at the time, remembers a rather more formal quip from Hutchence: 'I saw Michael go by and heard him whisper "Do we go out to dinner or just get married?"'

Whatever Hutchence's opening line was, Kylie was flabbergasted. That naivety was not an act. 'I couldn't make the words come out of my mouth,' she says. 'I was too taken aback. I do remember that I kept thinking about him. I couldn't understand why he would pay attention to someone like me. I was like, here I am, so uncool and just a little thing and he's Michael Hutchence and fancy saying anything like that to me! But, you know, it was shocking and amusing and tantalising and humorous. And in a way, that was Michael.' A group of Michael's friends, who had been watching the encounter, were extremely amused. 'It was absolutely hilarious,' said one. 'The moment Michael saw her, he jumped up and started running at her with his arms waving, loudly making obscene suggestions.'

Perhaps unsurprisingly, nothing came of that encounter and it was not until they were both in Tokyo a year later that the two really began to get on. Kylie had gone to one of his concerts. 'I was in the audience and thought he was looking at me,' she says. 'Later on I realised he was very short-sighted and couldn't have seen a thing. It didn't matter. It made me feel good just thinking about it. I was backstage afterwards and somebody said, "Michael would like to meet you." We had a little chat and went back up to his hotel room with a bunch of people. And I was just this straight person at a rock 'n' roll party. So straight. I was sitting on his bed and he was asking if he could get me a drink and I kept saying, "Oh no, no, it's okay, I'm fine, thank you." His girlfriend Jonny was jealous because he was talking to me.'

On another occasion she recalled, 'The first time I met him, he was trying to chat me up and I was like, no. I had a boyfriend at the time and he had a girlfriend. Once we were seeing each other, he was like, "I was trying to get you to have a drink", and I didn't want to. But after much persuasion I said, 'All right, I'll have a Baileys,' because that didn't taste like alcohol. Then he met me after an INXS show and I had on white tights, see-through sandals and a good girl skirt. I was too naïve to think why he'd ever be interested in me … And then people went back to his hotel room and I went and saw things I'd never seen before.'

Kylie was about to see an awful lot more. When Michael Hutchence the musician is forgotten, memories of Michael Hutchence the lover will long linger on. Michael embodied sex. Every move he made, every decision he came to, everything but everything, involved sex. 'He would have put himself in a position with a rather unattractive-looking prostitute from Kings Cross without even thinking about it because it was perverse, it was dirty and it was risqué,' says Nick Egan. 'Knowing Michael, it was always something other than the straight missionary position. There may have been hidden cameras in the room. There may have been another person involved. There may have been two other people involved. There may have been three girls and him. I mean I know, all that kind of stuff happened.'

Michael's fondness for what might be called multi-person sex is confirmed by another friend, Greg Perano. 'The way he indulged himself sexually was likely to be with a quantity of women,' he says. 'He liked having more than one partner at a time. He did like to spend hours surrounded by attractive women. He was like, you know, the knight who rides off and slays all these dragons and comes home with the beautiful princess and everyone goes, "Fantastic."' Or in Michael's cases, princesses. And if truth be told, it's hard to imagine Michael as a knight in shining armour – the more obvious comparison is with Lord Byron, the poet who was, 'mad, bad and dangerous to know'.

Greg also remembers that Michael suffered from a nihilistic streak, a trait that should perhaps have forewarned his friends that the rock star was likely to come to an untimely and mysterious end. 'I remember one night that we [spent] about two hours riding around on his motorbike around the parking lot and seeing how close we could come to walls,' he recalls. 'Then we had three people on the motorbike and I looked in his eyes that night. You could see that if he rode his motorbike into the wall and killed himself, it wouldn't have worried him.'

This was very strong stuff for a little girl best known for playing a garage mechanic and squeaking about how lucky she should be. But Kylie was ready for a change. Paul Flynn, the editor of *Attitude* magazine, sheds a little more light on the nature of their relationship by observing that Kylie was quite as willing to be corrupted as Michael was to corrupt her. 'I knew her stylist, Will, in Manchester,' he says. 'Will got the impression from Kylie that Michael Hutchence was an arch seducer just the way she talks about him. It seems as though Kylie and Jason had had an extremely innocent relationship and that she was gagging to shag Michael.'

She might well have been but Kylie also had the sense to play it cool. In those very early days, when she rang Michael a couple of days after the party in the hotel room and told him she would be in Hong Kong the next day, he assured her that by an extraordinary coincidence he would be there too and asked if he could take her out. 'What I didn't know was that he'd been told I was coming and had travelled to Hong Kong especially,' she says. The next day they met up. 'We went out and must have stayed talking in the streets of Hong Kong till four or five in the morning,' she recalls. 'We just hit it off amazingly well. But I wouldn't let him kiss me, which probably drove him crazy. After that he started sending flowers and there were constant telephone calls. Then we started going out. I just remember him treating me so well. He did throughout our entire relationship.'

There was just one problem. Kylie still had a boyfriend: one Jason Donovan. Up until then it had been Jason who dropped hints about looking around elsewhere: now, to his utter disbelief, he was seeing reports in the papers about Kylie and Michael. As usual Kylie and Jason were on opposite sides of the world so he couldn't confront her personally: worse still, for the first time ever, she was avoiding his phone calls and then neglecting to ring him back. But Kylie knew this approach could not continue forever. Matters finally reached a head a fortnight after she and Michael linked up: she finally rang Jason in New York and confessed that she was seeing someone else.

Jason was devastated. Although he had been the one who was so coy about confirming their relationship to the outside world, the one who had been so confident that Kylie would wait until the day he was ready to settle down – if, indeed, that day ever came – he suddenly and belatedly realised that Kylie was the woman he wanted. It was too late. Kylie was being introduced to a whole new world by Michael and there was no going back; soon she dismissed the four years she and Jason had spent together as 'a childhood relationship'.

Jason's hurt and anger soon turned to bitterness. Shortly afterwards, he went on the Australian television programme *Hey Hey, It's Saturday*, to review a pile of singles and used the occasion to make his feelings about his ex quite clear. 'And to think, this girl could have been my sister-in-law,' he snapped, holding up a picture of Dannii Minogue. 'I guess I'll have to grow my hair longer' – a reference, apparently, to Michael's long and unkempt locks. But he wasn't the only one to be wrong-footed by Kylie: Dannii was taken aback by her sister's new choice of partner too. 'When she told me, I was shocked,' she says. 'I couldn't picture them together.'

Initially, Kylie was extremely coy about the romance, just as she had been with Jason. 'At this stage we are just friendly,' she said shortly after she and INXS's singer had got together. 'I don't know if it'll develop in to something serious, we'll just see how we go.' And after admitting he made her happy, she added, 'But then it sounds like I met him and my whole life changed. I have met other people as well but Michael is a great friend and very under-standing. Performers look at other performers in a different way than the public do. You know that they are not immortal, they are real. They could be like the image they portray, or nothing like it. We just met and got along really well, we will just see what happens. It is nice having someone like Michael I can call up.'

Michael himself was in heaven as he basked in his unlikely conquest. 'It's very weird but Kylie's really got to me,' he said at the time. 'It's like some sort of spell which has made me feel all soppy. We've known each other at a distance for years but suddenly it's like seeing someone through different eyes. People who think we're ill matched don't know the real Kylie. I guess we might look a little odd together – I mean, I'm almost six feet and she's just over five feet. But there's nothing I wouldn't do for Kylie. I'm so proud of her. She's simply gorgeous.'

It was 1989, the end of the decade that was synonymous with excess and there was no better companion for Kylie with which to party the year out in style. And she wanted to: years later she remarked that if Michael hadn't been there to show her the seamier side of life, she'd probably have found it anyway. Like the character of Sandy in *Grease*, her heroine Olivia Newton-John's most famous role, Kylie was about to swap her girl-next-door image for that of a vamp. And she couldn't wait.

'I'm a fatalist; that's the time I was meant to meet him,' she said, looking back years later. 'I was meant to blossom and learn a bit more about the world. And I can't think of a better person to do it with. Similarly, he was going out with me – a really young woman – and it was almost too much for him to see that nearly every day I'd learn something. I was changing and learning and blossoming right in front of him. It was almost frightening to him – although frightening's not the right word, he loved it. But at the same time it is strange to see someone absorbing all they can. He just held my hand and took me on a trip to parts of the world I didn't know existed.'

The change was almost instantaneous. Although her features remained the same, the way Kylie presented herself altered dramatically: no longer the ingénue, she soon became a woman of the world. Kylie adored Michael, adored her new image and adored her new life and, fittingly for someone who has grown up so much in the public eye, that change was visible through an abrupt change of direction in her videos. The bubbly-haired soap star was replaced overnight by a sex siren, and whereas Kylie had formerly been jolly and girly, now she was sexy and sultry. Her mouth seemed to grow larger; her eyes took on a more knowing look. Kylie had been, if not exactly corrupted, then initiated into a very different world. And she loved it.

'There was this story with the ring I have on my finger in "Better The Devil You Know",' Kylie said in *The Kylie Videodrome*, a round-up of her videos, referring to the song that was her first release after meeting Michael. 'It was a ring that was Michael's and I think a fan gave it to Michael or a fan made it for him. It was just silver and it had an "M" on it and he – and I – used to wear it. We had just started going out then and you see the difference.

'There are videos from the start of my career and then it goes to "Hello, what has happened? There has been a big change in this girl's life." And it was him and it's just one of those little things that you do. I wanted to get my little personal thing in there, you know? That song, that video, that time was a big turning point for me.' The video, incidentally, caused uproar when it was released, not least because it features Kylie being fondled by a man practically twice her size. Kylie was scantily clad and the man was black; it shouldn't have caused such a fuss but it did. But then, everything Kylie did was starting to cause an uproar. She has often referred to the fact that she grew up in front of her audience; well, here she was entering late adolescence and to the stunned horror of everyone, discovering sex. Better the devil you know? Kylie was all out for new experiences and as eager as a young child to find out what was waiting for her in the great outside. She was soon to find out.

And Michael didn't just inspire Kylie to change her image. Of all unlikely people, he inspired Pete Waterman to write a song, too. '"Better The Devil You Know" was actually inspired by Kylie's relationship with Hutchence, although he never actually hung around the studio with her or anything,' Waterman wrote in his autobiography *I Wish I Was Me*. 'She rang me up at this time and asked if I'd help shield her from the press so she came up and stayed with me in Cheshire and we went horse riding and stuff together. Of course, the paparazzi wouldn't give up and we had to put up with photographers falling out of trees and falling through hedges, left, right and centre.' It was a small price to pay. Kylie was massively, helplessly, head over heels in love.

6

The Lord Byron
Of Rock

Kylie Minogue and Michael Hutchence could not have been more different. Michael was born in Sydney on 20 January 1960 and spent his childhood in Hong Kong. When he was 12, the family moved back to Australia, but three years later, after the separation of his parents, Michael moved to California with his mother, where by all accounts he was rather a lonely child – a condition that was not helped by severe acne (a legacy that remained as an adult in the form of his pock-marked skin).

The rows between his parents had also taken their toll on the young boy. 'I was very shy as a kid and looking back I'd say it was because of all the problems going on at home,' he once revealed. 'I don't understand couples who stay together for the sake of the family. It's incredibly upsetting – I know because I've been through it. At that time I was so shy I hardly spoke. I had spots and felt I was absolutely grotesque. I'm still shy and I hate people commenting on my looks because I still consider myself to be fairly ugly.'

Three years later, when Michael was 17, he moved back to

Australia and broke free of his childhood demons when he formed a band called The Fariss Brothers with three school friends, a band that was later to rename itself INXS. The name couldn't have been more apt. 'The good, sensible, rock and roll thing to do is to be completely drunk, take drugs and have sex all day,' Michael announced, shortly before his death in 1997 at the age of 37. 'I've led a much more decadent life than I've let on for a long time.' He wasn't exaggerating. 'Michael had this incredible power over women,' revealed one friend, 'They would do anything for him.' A friend of the Danish model Helena Christensen, Kylie's successor, recalled a night he spent with the couple.

'Helena was always asking what everyone's fantasies were,' he said. 'She said Michael used to ask her. One night she invited me and my girlfriend to dinner with them. We had room service in the Halkin Hotel in their suite. We had a real laugh but then there was this sudden change in the atmosphere and I thought things were going to get heavy any minute, so I left. It felt like anything could happen in that room and I didn't want to be a part of it. I'll never forget that night.'

Bill Leibowitz, a New York-based lawyer who worked with INXS, also remembers Michael's extraordinary powers over women. 'He projected what I call the triple S threat: sincerity, sensitivity and sensuality. Add to that his incredible voice, charisma, stage moves and the fact that he was a great-looking guy and women just found him completely irresistible. When I'm on an aeroplane, I can't even get a stewardess to get me a Coca-Cola. Michael blinks and he's in the restroom with her.'

Michael's life was dominated by sex; indeed, it is likely that it proved to be his undoing. He was found dead in a Sydney hotel room in 1997, hanging by a belt from the back of the hotel door and to this day it is a matter of debate as to whether he meant to commit suicide. His last partner and the last love of his life, the late television presenter Paula Yates, was adamant that it had been an accident caused by an experiment in auto-erotic asphyxiation. Certainly, there was a dangerous quality to Michael and that, combined with a very high sex drive, proved to be too unnerving for some.

But it wasn't all sex. Michael found time for other vices as well. Drink featured largely and he experimented with every drug known to man, including ecstasy, cocaine and heroin. Now he had the sex, drugs and rock 'n' roll lifestyle – and by the end of the 1980s, a decade now regarded generally as an era of conspicuous indulgence, he had Kylie, too. The world watched agog as he set about transforming her into a sex symbol.

'It's something no one ever expected – me as well,' said Kylie at the time. 'I'd love to be a fly on the wall and hear people's conversations about us. Obviously it is a difficult situation. We're both working in a similar field. It's very demanding, it's difficult. But it's also good.'

Michael lost no time in indulging in his new hobby. Drink, drugs, kinky sex – nothing was too much for his new amour. Clean-living Kylie tried to resist the drugs, but didn't last long and was soon giving interviews about her new recreational habits. 'It can be fun and it can be dangerous,' she said. 'I'm all for kids not taking drugs. But I don't want to say to them "You should never try anything."' This provoked absolute uproar at the time: any pop star who is unwise enough to enter into the big drugs debate tends to get blasted from all sides. In this case the outrage was even greater because the comments were coming from little Kylie, no less, who so many people still saw as Charlene from *Neighbours*.

Kylie didn't care; she was revelling in her new life. Next she posed for a set of nude pictures, pictures she herself commissioned from photographer Grant Matthews. 'I guess she wanted to do it,' said a bemused Grant. 'You're not 22 for ever.' As a matter of fact there was subsequently some discussion about those pictures appearing in a book, which would have had some similarities to Madonna's later book Sex. They never did, though and have not been published to this day.

When Kylie attended the Sydney premiere of *The Delinquents* with Hutchence in December 1989, the change in her appearance – in fact, her lifestyle – was evident for all to see. Arriving in a 1950s Cadillac, the couple caused a storm as they emerged from the car. Gone were the long curly locks of Kylie's previous incarnation: in its place was a platinum blonde bob (which later turned out to be a wig). Kylie wore a dress that just about made it down over her hips: Michael was equally outrageously clad in a waistcoat – no shirt – floral trousers and heavy workmen's boots. And he was happy to speak openly to the press about his new relationship.

'We obviously have a great affection for each other,' he said. 'We have a really good time.' And was there marriage in the air? 'There are no plans to get married,' said Michael hastily. 'We are simply enjoying ourselves. I am just happy for Kylie to know the premiere went so very well. Kylie is obviously to be taken very seriously as an actress from now on' – which either goes to show that Michael hadn't actually seen the film or that he had a much better sense of humour than he is usually credited with. Or that love really is blind, after all.

And Michael's family approved of his new choice of girlfriend, as well. 'She's a great kid,' said his father, Kelland.

'They seem very much in love.' And this from his mother Patricia: 'I think she's a very cute little girl – she's pretty smart. There's no doubt he's in love.'

Kylie had had two relationships before Hutchence, but this one was clearly something else. Tales abounded of their wild lifestyle, their days beginning in the evening, encompassing half the nightclubs of South-East Asia and not winding down until well into the following morning. Handcuffs were found in Kylie's luggage by outraged airport officials and the two were said to have had sex just about everywhere, including on that aeroplane mentioned earlier. 'A friend of Michael's repeated a story that Michael had told him and I think it was out of place for him to be talking about it,' said a rather embarrassed Kylie some years later. 'There was some truth to it but his story wasn't exactly correct.'

Nick Egan also spoke openly about their drug use, which could be dangerous in more ways than one, as became apparent when he recalled one extremely risky occasion that Michael enjoyed talking about. 'He liked to tell the story of when he was out with Kylie in the country,' he said. 'They had taken liquid ecstasy with a guy who was some hooray In England who was a marksman, and Kylie was sniffing a rose. The guy shot the rose from under her nose so it blew up in her face. Michael got a certain thrill and fear from that.'

The Australian author Dino Scatena also alleges that Kylie eventually decided to try drugs in her new life. 'It took a while to convince Kylie that a bit of dope or an ecstasy tablet wouldn't kill her,' he wrote. 'Kylie soon relented. The pair would become regular early-morning fixtures in a handful of Sydney's trendiest nightclubs. On some outings Kylie would look the worse for wear, stumbling downstairs, crashing out on lounges.'

Then there were rumours that the two had attended a massage parlour in Hong Kong together, followed by worldwide shock when Kylie suggested she could become a mother without getting married first. 'Yes, I do want to become a mum,' she announced. 'But I might well go ahead and have kids without being a wife!' Her fans reeled. Where had the sweet little TV star who threatened no one gone? 'I've been thinking that I don't want to reach 25 and think, Oh God, what happened to me since I was a teenager? Where has it all gone?' she explained. 'I want to enjoy myself as well. It's good to shock people. I like to do what people don't expect.'

She was certainly managing that. It was hardly surprising, though, looking back on her behaviour, that Kylie was breaking out of the confines of her old life. Over the previous couple of years, she'd been giving numerous interviews about how exhausted she was and how much she needed a rest; now here was Mr Indulgence in person, telling her to stop working and come out to play. (Not that she ever stopped altogether – even throughout her time with Michael, Kylie's career remained supremely important to her.)

It's worth bearing in mind that she had never had a teenage rebellion. When everyone else was smoking behind the bike sheds and getting told off for coming home late, sensible little Kylie was working. And working. And working … So in the long run, it was probably just as well for her mental well-being that Kylie was finally breaking out. She herself was the first to acknowledge a distinct change in her behaviour. 'Michael has influenced me tremendously,' she confessed at the time. 'He encourages me to be outrageous and just to go for it. He has given me a lot of confidence. Before we met I was very reserved but now I'm not. I have changed an incredible amount in the last year and grown up a lot. Much of that is down to Michael.'

But while you can take the girl out of the suburbs, you can't take the suburbs out of the girl. Kylie threw a party for Michael's thirtieth birthday: 100 friends gathered in a photographer's studio and feasted on champagne and home-baked chocolate cake, while Kylie led the pack in a rousing rendition of 'Happy Birthday', with Dannii beating time on a drum. The couple then drove off on Michael's Harley Davidson to another party at his apartment where it is fair to assume that something a little stronger than cake was on the menu.

Michael sometimes seemed as bemused by the relationship as everyone else. 'I used to be a Kylie knocker, hated what she stood for, never watched *Neighbours*,' he said in one interview (during which the interviewer noted he sniffed a lot and said very little). 'Let's just say I had a change of heart.'

But unlike so many others at the time, Michael saw a different Kylie (some might say he created a different Kylie) from the bubbly, boring little Charlene. 'She's very underestimated,' he argued. 'She's not at all the wimpish personality people think she is. She's very intelligent and deep, knows how to take care of business and works hard. I admire her for all the crap she's gone through and come out of it so strong. We're an unlikely couple, that's for sure.

'We're not exactly the same sort of people, it's true. Kylie comes from a different side of the tracks. She's lived a fairly cocooned sort of life. I'm influencing her, I guess. I've been around one way and another, most people have who are getting on for 30. Kylie is – or *was* – a straight girl.'

'He was totally charismatic and intelligent, witty and funny and filthy,' Kylie reflected fondly years later. 'But what was amazing was that he really let me be myself. He just loved me unconditionally. It was consistent to the end. I remember doing a secret warm-up gig in a small club. I was nervous but he was so proud of me. He took a back seat and let me shine.'

And for quite a while, the odd couple's relationship flourished. Next on the agenda were plans, sadly never realised, for a £1-million TV movie in which Hutchence would play a priest who falls for the charms of the young Kylie – the very role that Kylie had talked about a couple of years earlier. 'I'm serious,' said Michael to universal guffaws. 'The script is just about ready and we hope to start shooting in the second half of next year. We're both excited about it.'

And he wrote a song for her – 'Suicide Blonde'. 'Kylie dyed her hair this colour she called suicide blonde,' he recalled later. 'She said, "I'm going to go suicide blonde today." I think she was thinking of people like Marilyn Monroe and I thought it was a good name.' That's not all he thought was good about the petite one. 'She's the best fuck in the world,' he announced breezily on another occasion.

But even with a prize like Kylie on his arm, Michael was unable to curb his womanising ways. Rumours that he was being unfaithful while on tour filtered back to the petite chanteuse, followed by gossip that he was seeing not one but three other women – two old flames in the shape of Cathy Lee and model Rosanna Klitzner and the *home and away* actress Justine Clarke. Kylie was not amused and the liaison came to an abrupt, if temporary, end in May 1990. 'We no longer have a relationship,' she snapped. For now, that was it. Kylie really was in love and it wasn't long before rumours of a split were denied and the relationship was back on the road again. It seemed that she just could not resist the extraordinary new vistas Michael had opened up to her.

'I was 21 when I started dating Michael and I've always said it was like I had blinkers on and he took them off,' said Kylie. 'We went out for about 18 months but it seemed a lot longer. It was very intense and wonderful and it drove my manager crazy because Michael and I used to meet all over the place. I used to get my manager to shimmy things along so I could go to Frankfurt one weekend then fly off to Hong Kong ... Michael was such an amazingly charismatic, smart, well-read, wild poetic man. The press loved all that, of course, and it's easier if you're seeing someone who's used to it. If you see someone who isn't, it's a lot trickier. I have to put up with that media stuff, but my friends and family and boyfriend shouldn't.'

Her boyfriend at that time certainly used to get irritated by press attention. Gallingly for someone who had always occupied the limelight by himself, he found he was now getting as much attention for his relationship with Kylie as he was for his music, if not more, and that worse still, Kylie seemed to be even more popular with the media than he was. However, Michael tried to see the lighter side. 'I'm going to rename the band Mr Kylie Minogue and four other guys,' he said lightheartedly. Truth be told, the band was no longer the force in music it had once been. INXS's classic rock sound was as synonymous with the late 1980s as Kylie's Charlene. Like Kylie, Michael was also making a transition in the way he was perceived: from rock musician to legendary lover.

Still, he was not always so sanguine about the interest that existed in him purely as a result of his relationship with Kylie. 'It's horrible when people come over and they don't even acknowledge you,' he said. 'I now see it from a completely different point of view and I sympathise with anyone I've been with in the past. You get lots of people talking to you and then looking over your shoulder at Kylie.

Maybe they're straining to catch a glimpse of her because she's so small.'

However, despite numerous rumours that the couple had just – or were about to – tie the knot, the relationship finally came to an end in February 1991. Michael's womanising was becoming an increasing source of distress to Kylie, and he was increasingly linked to two other women: Patsy Kensit, who had publicly shoved her hand down his trousers in order to see if it was true that he had what Paula Yates later referred to as the Taj Mahal of crotches, and the beautiful 19-year-old Danish model Helena Christensen. The split happened when INXS were on tour: ironically, Michael ended it in just the manner Kylie had adopted with Jason Donovan – namely, on the phone. And Kylie had been doing a fair bit of telephoning herself, which was causing an increasing amount of friction.

'She often had trouble getting through to his hotel,' said a friend at the time. 'Then he'd be either out or half asleep and not in the mood. She usually ended up getting angry and the phone calls turned into bitter arguments. In the end Mike told her it was best if they called it a day. She's heartbroken because she still really loves the guy. Kylie's devastated, but at least she's not alone now. She's been seeing her old *Neighbours* pals like Jason Donovan.'

An INXS spokesman confirmed the split. 'Their conversations usually ended up with her accusing him of having a good time while she was all alone feeling miserable. Mike thought it was the best for the both of them. He still thinks the world of Kylie but he doesn't want to be responsible for causing her any more pain.'

But there were also rumours that Kylie herself had been out with other men, not least with the actor Marcus Graham who, confusingly, had been previously attached to Nicole Kidman, who went on to become the new Mrs Tom Cruise. Photographer Steve Dupont claimed to have taken snaps of the couple kissing in Sydney's Freezer nightclub, before two heavies, 'put an arm round my throat,' swore at him and told him to hand the film over. 'Before I could answer, they threw me against a wall and ripped the film out,' he recalled.

There is no doubt, though, that Kylie was devastated by the end of the relationship. 'I was so hurt when we broke up because I was very much in love with him,' she said sadly some years later. 'I spent a good part of the time crying my heart out.'

That was not the full story. Michael had never been good at ending his relationships outright and he allowed the situation to drift with Kylie for some time before finally bringing it to an end. Many people believe that Kylie has never really gotten over it and she was certainly left bewildered by the fact that it had all come to an end. 'It was one of those situations where you're not too sure why you broke up, but you did. We broke up on the phone. I flew to Manhattan so we could talk. He was very strange at that point and I remember him being somewhere that I'd never seen him before. He was just very distressed. I don't know what he'd been taking or what he'd really been going through, but he was not together.' In fact, Michael had already been with Helena Christensen for three months at this point.

Very unusually for him, Michael felt guilty about the way he'd treated Kylie, even telling his father Kelland, 'I let her down.' And there is no sign that Kylie is over it to this day, no matter how many boyfriends she's had since then. 'He was my first great love and it caused great heartbreak when we split up,' she says. 'I think he eventually wondered why it happened. We had a good thing and I'm sure he never ever wanted to hurt me. Maybe he indulged himself in too many projects, whether it be seducing women or reading poetry, taking drugs or staying in the most exquisite hotels. He was the first person I had been extremely close to who has died. But I'm sure he's laughing, looking down now, knowing that he's still teaching me.'

Kylie was devastated by Michael's death in November 1997. She was, however, able to joke about his funeral. 'There was always a lot of talk about Michael and his wicked ways,' she says. 'The bad boy of rock and all that. He was very Byronesque and I remember smiling at his funeral because as the coffin came out the thunder and rain started right on cue. You couldn't have scripted it better. He was just a very funny, educated, down-to-earth, hedonistic man. In truth I'm not sure that he corrupted me ... but let's just say that he opened my eyes to the ways of the world that I had not yet experienced. I would not have missed our relationship for anything and I miss him.'

Kylie still believes they are in touch. 'I don't know where he is most of the time unless he visits,' she says. 'I haven't for a little while, but I do and I did on the morning of his funeral. I've never gone into it in detail because it's too personal but I had a real amazing experience – just a feeling and a reaction in my body. I felt he was saying, "It's OK." It wasn't goodbye. It was comforting. I feel really lucky and thankful when he comes by.'

7

After He'd Gone

Kylie Minogue's life can be divided into two halves: Before Michael and After Michael. BM Kylie was a cute little girl next door; AM she became the world's leading sex kitten, a role that, despite the fact that she's nearing her mid-thirties, she still plays to this day. These days she can laugh at it – 'My so-called sexiness is more like a Carry On film,' she insists – but in the months after Michael left, Kylie didn't much feel like laughing at anything.

Life had to go on, though, and so Kylie did what she had always done: she threw herself into her work. And gradually, as it must, the pain began to diminish and Kylie found herself, to her own enormous astonishment, lusted after the world over. Much has been made in recent years of Kylie's relationship with hot pants, particularly the gold pair she wore in the video for 'Spinning Around'. More of those hot pants – much more – later. But it was actually back then, right at the beginning of the 1990s, that Kylie began making the most of her pertest asset. She posed wearing nothing but a pair of pink ostrich hot pants – her second pair, after donning some of the silver Lycra variety for 'Better The Devil You Know' a year earlier – and looked absolutely magnificent.

'I have reached the stage in my life where I am a girl-woman,' declared Kylie (she was actually 23 at the time). 'I felt like Brigitte Bardot while the photos were being taken. I had such fun jumping up and down on the bed, humming to Marilyn Monroe, who was singing in the background. I think being a girl-woman is very appealing and has a lot of sexuality.' And did she think she was sexy? 'I wouldn't describe myself as sexy,' she replied, consigning herself to a minority of one. 'Sexy is raunchy. I think people can see there is a sexuality about me but it doesn't mean I'm trying to be sexy.'

What it might have meant was that Kylie was beginning to realise that if she wanted to stay on top of the pop world, she would have to become as chameleon a performer as that other petite blonde who has not only defied but outlasted all her critics: Madonna. Kylie had already had one sensational image change, courtesy of Michael Hutchence, which had done her no harm at all and clearly made her aware of the fact that there is mileage in surprising people by the way you look. Today it was pink ostrich feathers, and tomorrow – who knows? 'I rapidly get bored with the way I look and I reckon if I am, everyone else must be,' she said at the time. 'I love changing myself.

'The nice girl image got me started and successful, but it would be a lie to pretend to be that now. I decided to get rid of that image 18 months ago, but when I started to make changes, people said, "What are you doing?" and "Where's your frilly frock?" I was surprised at how shocked they were. People have been saying about me, "She's grown up" and sounding surprised, as if they thought that wasn't going to happen.' She was also developing an acute sense of style that was to stand her in very good stead in the years to come. 'Most of my clothes are second hand,' she said (the famous gold hot pants included). 'I like a bargain and it also makes sure I have something no one else has.'

It is telling that even back then, Kylie was very aware of the comparison with Madonna, and not just in a musical sense. 'Madonna has been a great inspiration not only with my work but because she is also a great business woman,' she admitted. 'But I don't want to be a new Madonna and I have tried not to model myself on her. I want to develop my own style. But I do like the way she changes her image. And if she can do it, so can I.'

It was not just in music and image that Kylie was taking on a new view of the world. AM, Kylie's attitude to life generally had changed and she was beginning to emerge as a very much more sophisticated version of her former self. For starters, she stopped being a vegetarian – 'I'm much healthier now' – and although not a smoker herself, refused to start acting the puritan. 'It's wrong to say I have banned smoking on my tours,' she protested. 'I don't mind other people smoking around me at all.'

Kylie was also beginning to develop a sense of herself as an artist in a way she hadn't previously, when she allowed everyone around her to make decisions for her. 'I know the bottom line is to sell records and there is a certain amount of packaging,' she said. 'I also know record companies want you to adapt yourself to suit the audience, but I am changing my audience to suit me. I see myself as two people: one is Kylie Minogue Enterprises Ltd and the other is me. I know my image is my lifestyle, but it's also my life.

'I now consider myself an artist. I want to express how I feel and look how I want to look, rather than what other people want me to be like. When I was in *Neighbours*, I tried to please everyone else, but now I do things my way or not at all. I'm taken a lot more seriously now and have become a lot more confident, but hopefully I won't turn into a monster. My confidence has come with age. I love the way I say that as if I am 35! I now smile at my naivety. It will never happen again.'

Kylie's attitude to the rest of her life was changing, as well. Michael had taught her how to have fun and now she intended to do just that. 'I have worked flat out for years but after I toured Australia and Japan this February and March, I said that if I didn't have a break, I wouldn't do anything. It's something I'd never have said a few years ago.' Kylie nipped off to Paris for a while, where she took stock of her life. 'I'm always assessing myself,' she revealed. 'No one could be more critical of me than I am. But I don't like looking back. I get embarrassed and sometimes think, Why didn't someone stop me from doing that? I like to look forward.

'When I was doing *Neighbours*,' she reflected, 'I didn't know how to enjoy myself and relax. I worked all the time and I had to learn how to be sociable. When I was 19 and meeting someone socially, I would shake hands as if I were at a business meeting. Now I think it is just as important to make time to enjoy myself as it is to be good at my job because they complement each other. It was wonderful to slow down, sit in cafes, see friends and do a lot of nothing. Now I know I have to look after myself and be true to myself because in turn I am much better for everyone else. I'm a much happier person than I used to be.'

There may have been another reason for that. Kylie had just filmed the video 'What Do I Have To Do?' and had been spotted kissing 25-year-old South African model Zane

O'Donnell, who had appeared in the shoot. Were they an item? 'No,' she said firmly, 'he was just in my video.'

For now, that was. It was four months after the split and Kylie was waking up again. She had made headlines with Michael and now she began to do exactly the same with Zane – who rapidly did become her boyfriend – not least because of his complicated past. For a start, Zane O'Donell has a son, then aged five, by his ex-wife, Lauren, a year his junior.

Zane, like Michael, was a man with an eye for women. When he first started dating Kylie, he was still seeing the German model Daria Lingenberg, which led to various warnings about Kylie's new man. The first to speak up, perhaps unsurprisingly, was Zane's ex-wife Lauren: 'The only way Kylie will stop him going off with other women is to castrate him,' she stated. 'She'd better beware. Zane broke my heart because he can't resist beautiful women. We got married when I was 18 and lived in New York, In Milan and in London. We both enjoyed the bright lights, but he made me very unhappy. He was always off with other girls.

'I didn't know it at first, then I found out about one girl. When I confronted him, he denied it. I gave him a chance but then I found out there had been lots of other girls all the time.' He broke my heart but it is for the best because I've a more stable relationship now. I'm getting married in November and my boyfriend has promised he will treat my son as his own.'

The next to speak up was German model Daria Lingenberg. Zane, it appeared, had been living with her for 10 months and had forgotten to mention the fact that he was going out with Kylie to his erstwhile girlfriend. 'I know he and Kylie are friends, but he is going out with me,' she said. 'We have been together for nearly a year.'

Zane's mother Sandra, who was based in Cape Town, added to the confusion. 'I hardly know who Kylie Minogue is, but I knew that he had been seeing her, because he made a video with her,' she said. 'I'm surprised, because the last I heard he was living in Paris with Daria. Then he suddenly moved to London. Now we know why. Girls won't leave him alone and it causes pressure on relationships. All the girls are so mad about him. He really loved his wife but she got tired of women chasing him.'

'I'm having a great time,' said Kylie, who was clearly determined to put a brave face on her hurt over losing Michael. 'I guess it's true that I've discovered sex. I've learned to relax.' And as for any other girlfriends, Kylie soon saw off the competition. 'Kylie knows everything and they sorted it all out between them,' said a friend at the time. 'She's been seeing more and more of Zane and he took her out for her birthday last week. She's really happy.'

The relationship was to last for a year, but finally fell apart after a series of rows prompted by Zane's roving eye. The last straw was, ironically, a video shoot during the course of which Zane was seen getting amorous with Brigitte Slama, a French dancer. Kylie had had enough and ended it. 'Kylie's very upset,' said a friend. 'She thought Zane might be Mr Right but his eye for the ladies got too much for her.' Well, maybe. But, it's more likely that Kylie had already met her Mr Right and, as it later emerged, was far from getting over him. 'It's much better to end a stagnant relationship than hang on,' was Kylie's own take on it. Perhaps prompted by the harm he had caused by his errant ways, Zane later became a born-again Christian.

Kylie hung on to some of the other habits she had cultivated during her time with Michael, most notably taking ecstasy. This was the early Nineties, after all, when the vast majority of twenty-somethings throughout Britain were working by day, clubbing by night and – to use the vernacular – getting off their heads in the process. Kylie was no different from anyone else and indulged herself with gusto, as she later admitted to an American magazine. 'I had my phase,' she said. 'When I was going out a lot, it was a great time in my life. We really got in to the dance culture. But we've become such prudes. Anyway, you're only meant to do ecstasy for a certain phase in your life. I enjoy work and know my day's going to be that much harder if I've wrecked myself the night before.'

In between relaxing, Kylie was beginning to take a much more hands-on approach to her career. In the early days, she was probably wise to let the masters of the art – Stock, Aitken and Waterman – tell her what to do, but she had been singing for a few years now and was beginning to have her own ideas. 'I was always made to wear primary colours and told to smile, smile, smile,' she says. 'I was put on the production line and came out as a prettily gift-wrapped box with probably not a lot in it. I was never consulted on anything. If I was lucky they might show me my new album cover, but they were not particularly interested in my opinion.'

Given that she wasn't encouraged to express her thoughts, Kylie did at least have one means of discovering her identity: through her clothes. Her first change of image came when she starred in *The Delinquents*, and while the film was terrible, the look wasn't. Kylie was beginning to learn. Next came the Hutchence years, in which she turned in to SexKylie, an image which, through a variety of permutations, exists to this day. Danny Kelly, then editor of *Q magazine*, noted, 'It's standard pop business stuff. You quickly become old hat and to keep your audience interested, you have to come up with something new.'

The editor of *Smash Hits* saw a more cunning plan. 'She was very clever,' he said. 'We all get embarrassed about the things we did when we were teenagers and she made sure that people knew that she had changed. She wants to be a megastar. She did not want embarrassing designs for record sleeves holding her back.'

Kylie herself saw her actions as a way of trying to take more control. 'I was really trying to put more of myself into my work,' she says today. 'Since I couldn't take control of the music side of things, I managed to get my image in my hands and use that. Looking back, I might have gone a little off the rails, taken things too far, but I had to get it out of my system. I was trying to say, "This is me. Hi! Look, look, I'm here." 'I think people liked her and rock journalists certainly thought she was a good thing,' says Danny Kelly. 'But it has to be said that it was probably a hormonal thing – rock journalists are all men.'

Casting around AM for another new image, Kylie decided to reinvent herself in the look of Madonna. Going on tour, Kylie wore a black body-piece and Madonna-style headset – not, it must be said, to universal acclaim. It was all very well reinventing yourself as many times as Madonna, but when you reinvent yourself as Madonna …

There was, however, one part of society that absolutely loved it, and that was the gay community. It was at about this time that Kylie really began to establish a fan base in gay clubs – after all, she'd been dumped by the love of her life and your average superstar has to suffer some kind of tragedy to become a gay icon – and they loved the new SexKylie. The compliment was returned in spades. 'I love performing to them,' says Kylie. 'They love my music and I love the fact that they do. They're a great audience but it can be such a struggle. They are so excitable but they have the vocal capacities of full-grown men. It can get so loud I can hardly hear myself sing.'

To show her appreciation of this particular element of her fan base, in 1991, Kylie appeared at Sydney's gay Mardi Gras (in previous years, it had been dominated by Kylie look-alikes). 'I felt I owed it to them because they supported me years before anybody else did,' she says. Her arrival was kept a secret and the audience only realised what was about to happen when 20 male dancers in hot pants bearing Kylie's initials leapt on stage. 'I was dressed in a baby doll dress and there were pyrotechnics all around me,' she says. 'It was hysteria.'

By 1992, Kylie's experimentation with different looks led to bizarre rumours growing up about her. First she appeared in a push-up top: 'Kylie has NOT had a breast implant,' snapped her agent Sue Foster. 'She doesn't believe in them. It's just the tops that she's wearing, they're more uplifting. Or maybe she's still developing, she's only 24.' Next she wore a figure-hugging dress. 'Kylie is NOT pregnant,' insisted Sue Foster. 'It would be impossible. She's not even had a boyfriend for months.'

And Kylie herself, now single again, was beginning to wonder if she would ever meet the right man. 'It isn't easy for me,' she said. 'Some guys who come up to me are real jerks, treating me as if we're friends when I don't know them. The sweet ones just nod and steer clear. I bet one of those guys is the one for me.'

Kylie also had a shocking experience when she was filming her video for 'Finer Feelings' in Paris: a man tried to commit suicide in front of her. She screamed as she saw a man throw himself in to the River Seine, before shouting to her crew to rescue him. 'It was horrifying,' she said. 'I was almost frozen with fear. One person dived in the water and the others rushed to get the police. The guy was saved from drowning and taken to hospital suffering from severe shock. It took us a long time before we could continue filming. That moment will stay with me forever.'

AM, life continued to move on. Kylie's younger brother Brendan attempted to launch a singing career in Sydney with the backing of both sisters, while Kylie was briefly reunited with Jason when both agreed to take part in the Rhythm of Life fashion show at London's Grosvenor House Hotel in aid of the Rainforest Foundation. This was to turn into something of an annus horribilus for Jason too, incidentally: it was the year that he went on to sue the magazine *The Face* for saying he was gay and while he won the case, he lost an enormous amount of friendship in the show biz community. Kylie, however, stuck up for her ex. 'I can categorically state that Jason is heterosexual,' said Kylie who, after all, should know. 'I think he's suing *The Face* because he doesn't want to spend the rest of his life saying, "It's not true." I don't know what I would have done but I do think it's unfair that he's had such a bad run over that.'

The demands of show business were taking their toll. Normally an absolute trouper, Kylie was now talking about a very different life. 'I often consider giving it all up,' she said wistfully. 'I'd like to study at university or maybe back-pack across Thailand. I went on holiday to Arizona recently and it blew my mind. I wasn't hassled – people just left me alone. There are times when I hate what I do and everything surrounding what I do. I don't like fame and recognition, the loss of a personal, private life. Sometimes I just want to be a normal girl.' There were rumours she was moving to Paris, rumours that were fuelled when she dressed as Brigitte Bardot in a new video.

Above: Happy families! In a rare picture of the talented Minogue family, Kylie is pictured with her sister Dannii, brother Brendan and mum Carol.

Below left: Kylie's proud grandmother, Brenda.

Below right: Kylie with her mum who eagerly watches every step of her daughters' successful showbusiness careers.

Above: Although Brendan is more accustomed to behind-the-scenes, this early photo shows him and Dannii singing at an after-show party for the Australian Logie TV awards.

Below: Kylie's family are very important to her. She is pictured here with her great uncle, *left*, and on the right, Kylie is pictured with a family of a different kind – *The Henderson Kids* was one of her first TV roles.

Above left: Kylie Minogue starred alongside Jason Donovan in *Neighbours*. As rumours surrounded their off-screen relationship, millions of people tuned in to see their characters Scott and Charlene get married.

Above right: Kylie eventually left the programme to pursue her career as a pop star. She is pictured here performing 'The Locomotion'.

Below: It wasn't long before the pair were reunited, this time to sing their smash hit single 'Especially for You'.

Above left: Many people were surprised when Kylie and Michael Hutchence began dating.

Above right: A distraught Kylie at Michael's funeral. It is thought that she still regards him as the greatest love of her life.

Below: Kylie chats to Paula Yates on the *Big Breakfast* in 1992. At the time of Michael's death, Paula was his lover.

Kylie is pictured here with Alice Cooper and Charlie Slatter. She appeared alongside Charlie in *The Delinquents*.

Kylie soon ventured into indie music as she released a duet with Nick Cave. Later, she collaborated with the band of the moment – The Scissor Sisters.

Kylie's infamous bottom makes an appearance at one of her concerts.

Kylie is Australia's sweetheart. Her image was projected onto the Sydney Harbour Bridge. She also enjoyed more high-profile advertising when her own idol, Madonna, wore a t-shirt bearing Kylie's name, *inset*.

Fat chance. Kylie continued to arouse interest everywhere she went and with everything she did. She was the subject of an attack by Viz magazine for reasons that have never been entirely clear and the subject of gossip when she filmed the video for 'What Kind of Fool' with model Rob English. 'Rob and Kylie are NOT an item,' snapped Sue Foster. 'They're just good friends.'

That single, followed by a greatest hits album, was to be her last with PWL. Even then, though, when Kylie was still with Stock, Aitken and Waterman, her music was beginning to evolve, another good reason for changing her look. 'The music was changing, better,' says Kylie, 'but the image was the only thing I truly had in my grasp. So it was like, "Right! Now I'm going to be Miss Vixen." I was going to rebel and do everything I hadn't been allowed to do before. But it was time for the music to catch up.'

Kylie was finally allowed to try her hand at a little song writing on her fourth album, *Let's Go To It* – 'Every little step forward to me was like a gold medal,' she says – but increasingly she was beginning to feel the need for a change. She decided to leave PWL. There was nothing to stop her: she had signed up for five albums, including a greatest hits, and with these out of the way she could go anywhere she wanted. PWL tried to tell her to stay, pointing out what they had achieved together. And they had a point: 'Everything we'd done together had been successful,' agrees Kylie.

'PWL had the attitude that they were the best. And in one sense, they made me.' And so she embarked on a tour to find a new label, with every record company worth its salt trying to persuade her to come on board: 'Many lunches and dinners,' she says. Her public profile fell slightly – 'I prefer it this way,' she said firmly, 'instead of people leering out of car windows and yelling obscenities at you.' But you know what they say: the only thing worse than being talked about is not being talked about. And anyway, Kylie was giving everyone plenty to talk about.

It was towards the end of 1992 that she first began to discuss doing a book (another book eventually appeared in 1999) full of pictures of herself, complete with no clothing. Madonna's book *Sex* had come out in the same year and Kylie was immediately accused of copying the idea. 'My book will be very sophisticated and the nude shots have all been done in a very subtle way,' she retorted. 'They are very discreet. I don't feel I'm imitating Madonna. I had the idea for doing naked pictures a long time ago. Besides, they won't dominate the book. There will be lots of pictures of me wearing some wonderful outfits. The pictures everyone sees of me usually show the cute Kylie, but these are different.'

As we noted before, the book never appeared – and it is entirely possible that Kylie decided not to go ahead when she saw the reaction to *Sex*. Madonna really had gone too far, by posing for pictures that left absolutely nothing to the imagination, leaving her public with absolutely nothing to wish for. Absolute derision followed and Madonna bowed out of the limelight for a time after that until all the fuss died down.

Kylie's looks continued to evolve. Now there was something else occupying the nation's thoughts: blessed with a naturally large mouth, Kylie's lips nonetheless seemed even bigger than ever. Had she had a lip job? 'Absolutely NOT,' snapped ... Kylie herself, actually. Clearly getting rather fed up with all the speculation about her appearance, she angrily announced that she was wearing make-up. She was also beginning to get a bit sick of the accusation that she was copying Madonna. 'I'm fed up with people saying I'm ripping her off,' she fumed. 'She's always learned from others. Everyone from Marilyn Monroe to Greta Garbo.'

For many years Kylie tried to escape her soap sudsy past, but right from the beginning it was a doomed hope, as Kylie was to learn. Towards the end of the year plans were mooted to scrap *Neighbours*: its two most famous ex-stars were called in to take up the programme's cause. '*Neighbours* was the start of my career and I feel very strongly about it,' said a good-natured Kylie. And a spokesman for Jason chipped in, 'He will certainly not want to see the end of *Neighbours* on British television.' The programme lived to see another day.

Kylie also had another shot at film stardom, with the movie *Street Fighter*, in which she starred with Jean-Claude Van Damme. Unfortunately, it fared no better than *The Delinquents*. 'There's little to get excited about in this laughably bad film adventure,' said one critic, and few would disagree.

She might have been quiet musically, but Kylie's love life was arousing quite as much interest as ever. It was at around this time that rumours arose linking her with Prince, soon to become The Artist Formerly Known As, one of the few pop stars in the world who could make Kylie look tall. In an interview she gave to *The Face*, Kylie describes how the two diminutive icons met and became friends. The two shared the same security people and so it was that she was taken backstage to meet him at a concert. Then she went to see him in his studio where 'there were a few jokes flying around.'

'Where do you want your mike set up!' he cried. 'Where are your lyrics! Come on!' Kylie gave him the lyrics to a song she'd written called 'Baby Doll': 'Sugar and spice and all things nice/Come and show me paradise/Let me be your baby doll.' (And they said Kylie was just a pretty face.) Prince took the lyrics, finished the song and sang it back to the petite chanteuse.

And so, asked *The Face*, how much did he know about you? 'I don't think he knew much, or at least he didn't let on. But he did mention one quote which I said some time back, about him being "Sex on a stick." Which is funny now that I know him.'

Next up, Kylie went to visit Prince in Paisley Park, his complex which includes both his house and a recording studio. 'I went to Minneapolis for a while and hung out there,' she related. 'In the studio. I'm sure my story could match many other girls' stories. To a point, I must add,' she added primly. 'The point before anything really interesting starts to happen.' When pressed on whether the pixie popster had amorous designs on her, Kylie diplomatically responded 'Not exactly', though she couldn't help but acknowledge that he is 'Famous for being fresh! But who wants to be on that list!' Clearly, though she respected the multi-talented Prince's musical savvy, she was not about to become another notch on the Paisley Park bedpost.

A trip to Prince's house had followed. And did he make a move on our heroine there? Well, not exactly: 'We had a game of table tennis.' And he absolutely wiped the floor with her. Then, for good measure, he thrashed her at pool too. She added that although she couldn't remember the final scores, 'I do remember doing a glorious flying leap, trying to do an almost impossible return and landing in the shagpile … that is my fondest memory of Prince.'

Meantime, Kylie wasn't neglecting her career. While in the States, she also did a tour of the movie studios in LA. 'I met casting agents and heads of studios,' she said. 'But their world is usually so small. It's not even America, just Hollywood, and they don't know who I am. I talk to them and I'm just another blonde bimbo coming in, and as they're talking about their new golf club set I'm thinking, I could be doing a European tour!' Her choice of leading man, she confided, would be Al Pacino or Sean Connery. 'I do have a thing for the older man...' As we know, she eventually ended up with a very different package altogether, in the form of Jean-Claude Van Damme.

Meanwhile, new avenues were opening up for Kylie all the time. She was informed about a short story by *Trainspotting* author Irvine Welsh. Called *Where The Debris Meets The Sea* and included in his collection *The Acid House*, the story concerns four women – Madonna, Victoria Principal, Kim Bassinger and Kylie Minogue – who sit around in a house in Santa Monica fantasising about unattainable manual workers from Leith. The same subject matter had been covered before – and a good deal better – when Peter Cook and Dudley Moore sat around in the guise of two pub bores talking about the famous women they've had to fight off – 'there was a tap on the window. It was bloody Greta Garbo, hanging on the window sill in a see-through nightie. I had to smash her down with a broomstick' – and this particular tale reeks of so much male fantasy you can practically smell the testosterone rising from the pages. But true to form, Kylie was as nice as she could be about the story.

'I still don't really know what to make of it,' she admitted. ' It's basically his ... sexual fantasies. I don't know if he's got the women – I don't think we were dissimilar to the Fat Slags [*Viz's* famous characters] in it. With good intentions.' She was too right there: Irvine, in one of the most blatant cases of wishful thinking ever committed to paper has 'Kylie' fantasising about visiting a Scottish nightclub called Clan: 'Imagine the cock in thair. Comin out the fuckin waws.' In your dreams, Irvine mate, but that's the price of stardom, having Scottish authors lusting after you in their prose, just as Kylie later had to put up with Frank Skinner drooling over her gold hot pants. Reading between the lines – hers, not Irvine's – she didn't really seem to be that impressed.

The Face bumped into Kylie again a few weeks later. In the intervening time, she had been to the Monte Carlo World Music Awards – and amongst those present were Prince, Michael Hutchence and Helena Christensen. First, Prince. Kylie revealed that she and Prince had slowdanced to one of his own songs, 'The Most Beautiful Girl In The World'. And Prince played the gentleman too. Well, almost … Kylie admitted that he had got a bit fresh, but added that, 'I think he's always a bit on the fresh side. He just is.'

'You should hear the music they play at that club,' she confided to the style magazine. 'Believe me, I dropped to my knees and thanked the Lord when Prince and his crew arrived, because they put on some decent music.' (Albeit, Prince's own stuff.)

And now on to Hutchence. There was a separate report at the time that Michael was utterly furious with Prince because the latter had tried to flirt with Helena two years earlier and had thus boycotted his party. Helena had been at Les Bains Douche nightclub with a friend, when Prince arrived and invited the two of them back to his hotel. They declined, but Michael went ballistic. 'Michael has never forgotten that night,' admitted a friend. 'He was livid with Prince for trying to flirt with Helena under his nose. Prince tried very hard to get Helena and her friend back to his place – I guess he thought they could have had a great party. Since then he has avoided Prince. When he was invited to Prince's show, Michael's answer was unprintable.' Kylie, however, was one of the revellers at the bash.

Diplomatic as ever, Kylie told *The Face* that her time in Monte Carlo had been 'a most eventful few days', what with the presence of a very famous ex-boyfriend around. The interviewer pressed her on the point, asking whether the rumours were true that she had altered her seat allocations on the plane so that she and Hutchence would not be sitting together. 'Not exactly,' she replied, before laughing and adding, 'Dot, dot, dot.'

Poor Kylie. That interview was given in the middle of 1994, three and a half years after the break up with Michael and, as it turned out, only a few months before Michael was to leave Helena for Paula Yates. But Kylie was clearly nowhere near over Michael, no matter how many men she'd cavorted with in between. Rock's wild man still had her in his power as he does, to a certain extent, to this very day.

By her own admission, Kylie has been in love since then, and currently seems to be happy in her romantic life, but Michael was and always will be the love of her life. And back then, in the early 1990s, the pain was clearly extremely raw. It was to be a long while before Kylie could even think about having another serious relationship again.

8

Indie Princess

Having left PWL, Kylie was on the hunt for a new record label. In retrospect the label she eventually chose to sign up with looks like a bizarre decision for a populist little singer from Australia but, as Kylie was after the credibility vote, it must have seemed like a good idea at the time. In April 1993, she linked up with deConstruction, an indie dance label, with a view to becoming hip and groovy rather than mainstream and clichéd (and popular). The new partners raved about one another. Kylie gushed, 'deConstruction have a brilliant reputation to uphold, so I'm kind of relying on their reputation rather than my own ... There were two options. Either we could make another pop record or we could throw me into the field and try just anything. We chose the latter.'

The duo behind deConstruction were equally optimistic. 'Kylie is regarded as a trashy disco singer,' said Pete Hatfield, co-founder of the label. 'We regard her as a potential radical dance diva.' 'We just think she's a complete star,' added his partner Keith Blackhurst. 'She's almost like a diva. We just thought the opportunity to work with Kylie, who'd obviously grown up, was an opportunity to have a star, in the true sense of the word, working with us and our team of creative people.'

Initially, Kylie was euphoric about her new life. 'I secretly love worry, I bring it on myself,' she subsequently admitted. 'Three months after I left PWL, I panicked. I kept thinking I was washed up, people were going to forget me.' But it had been time for a change. 'It was like finishing a marathon,' she says. 'I'd done five albums with them and I truly felt that our working relationship had gone as far as it possibly could.'

Kylie was touchingly delighted to be associated with so many hip and groovy artists, such as M People, Black Box, N-Jois and K-Klass – the only problem being that she had no idea who many of them were. M People was the exception: 'My heart starts to wobble when I hear them somewhere in the world,' she revealed at the time, 'and I think: Stablemates! and I get proud.'

But she was touchingly delighted by the reaction she was getting from her new friends in the industry. 'It baffles me how it happened but somehow people have been able to see through,' she said at the time. 'These people who have taken an interest in my career have been able to see that there are more ... possibilities. And to have someone's belief is wonderful. You can bloom with that.'

One person felt rather more dubious about Kylie's change of direction: Pete Waterman. 'Towards the end of the time she was working with us,' he wrote in *I Wish I Was Me*, 'she was discovering a whole load of new ambitions, setting her sights at becoming the new Prince or Madonna. What I found amazing was that she was outselling Madonna four to one, but still wanted to be her. Everyone wanted to be Kylie Minogue except Kylie Minogue, who wanted to be Madonna. On top of that, I think Kylie was getting embarrassed by her past because it was part of her growing up. She had to reject her past so she could find her own identity. I was fine about that, but it just meant that if she wanted to do something else, she'd have to do it with someone else.'

So she did. But Kylie soon found out that her new life was to be very different from the happy days at PWL. The deConstruction label was delighted with its new acquisition, but no one seemed to know exactly what to do with her. She started meeting people in the industry, including Primal Scream, The Beloved, St Etienne, Keith Allen and others too numerous to mention. 'When she first came into the studio, her voice was the sound of PWL,' says Steve Anderson, half of the team Brothers in Rhythm, who went on to produce Kylie's debut album with deConstruction. 'It had that nasal quality to it, the horrible Kylie Minogue quality that graced so many records. Throughout the course of recording the album, she gained confidence in her vocals and surprised herself with what she was able to do.'

SexKylie might have been a raunchy little rock chick, but still she seemed rather too salubrious for some of the company she was keeping. Bobby Gillespie, lead singer with Primal Scream, once distinguished himself by asking her how she felt about people masturbating over her. They chatted about working together before, according to Kylie, Bobby offered her 'all these delights being passed around: Jack Daniel's … etc.' Kylie had an orange juice. Then she met a couple of other members of the band. 'We were going to do a song from their album,' she says, 'but in a different way. I can't even think what it was, now.'

Meetings with many more people followed: a new album

was underway, although it was to be a long time before it saw the light of day after innumerable meetings, collaborations, cancellations and all kind of non PWL-style palaver. 'They're never going to let me stop,' said Kylie at the time. 'I'm on a treadmill. This thing not being quite there is dangling the carrot right in front of me. I want it to be finished so I can know what I'm talking about.'

She set about reshaping herself in a new image, not so much SexKylie as IndieKylie and was thus thoroughly irritated when Jason Donovan chose this moment to speak more openly about their relationship than he ever had done before. Radio 1 DJ Steve Wright asked him, on air, a very direct question: 'Did you sleep with Kylie?' Jason decided to tell all. 'You want to know the truth?' he asked. 'Yes, I did. We had a relationship for four years. We never turned round and blatantly said we were going out. But it was the whole bits and pieces, that's the diplomatic answer.'

Despite the fact that their relationship had been known about since 1988, that 'bits and pieces' comment was the first time Jason had ever admitted that theirs had been more than just a holding-hands relationship. It caused an absolute furore, was widely repeated elsewhere and made it into various 'Quotes of the week' sections. Kylie was livid. 'She can't believe Jason would just blurt this out in a radio interview with millions of listeners tuning in,' snapped a friend. 'They did go out a long time ago, but after they split up they had a pact between them that they would never discuss their relationship in public. So you can imagine how she felt when she was told Jason had admitted actually sleeping with her to Steve Wright. She's gone up the wall.' Actually, given that the relationship had been known about for some time, and since Kylie was trying to establish a new image for herself, it's far more likely that she was annoyed by being reminded of her *Neighbours* past.

A hint of what was to come in the Noughties appeared in the form of Robbie Williams, then part of teen sensation Take That. Kylie turned up to an aftershow party when the winsome fivesome had done a concert at Wembley, and impressed young Robbie no end: 'She's gorgeous and frail,' he burbled. 'You feel like you want to protect her and keep her under your wing. Unfortunately none of us are allowed girlfriends at the moment so we can only remain the best of friends.'

Evan Dando, lead singer of the Lemonheads, was rather luckier than Robbie. Evan and Kylie met at a nightclub in Melbourne and friends watched open-mouthed at what happened next. 'Kylie just looked at him across the room,' said one. 'You could feel the sexual energy crackling. They kissed openly in the nightclub, then she held on to his hand and led him into a cloakroom. It was a good hour before they emerged. Kylie's hair was all over the place. Both of them had beaming smiles.' 'We hung out for a couple of nights,' said Kylie lightly, 'so at least there's a reason for stories that we're boyfriend and girlfriend. Which we're not.'

It was a step forward, though, for there had been no one serious for Kylie since she'd split up with Zane. And finally, in September 1994, came the release of her new album, entitled *Kylie Minogue*. Kylie signified her more serious intentions by appearing in a pair of spectacles on the cover and the debut was a respectable performance: the preceding single 'Confide In Me' got to number two and the album reached number four, so there were, for the time being, satisfied faces all round.

Various singles from the album followed, of which the most notable was probably 'Put Yourself In My Place', not so much because of the music (it is about a woman who has never been able to get over her ex-lover, incidentally) but because of its accompanying video. 'The inspiration for it is *Barbarella*. I'm a massive fan of that film,' Kylie revealed at the time. For the uninitiated, *Barbarella* is a classic of its time, a 1960s film starring Jane Fonda as an extremely amorous astronautette who cavorts around space in possibly the least practical spacesuit ever envisaged, having … adventures. It has another link to the music world, incidentally, in that it features a character called Duran Duran, from which the 1980s group took its name.

Kylie's video features one theme alone: she enters the spacecraft clad in a fetching pink spacesuit and proceeds to disrobe while floating in a space capsule. Her clothes are whisked away in to the ether until she is left with nothing but a blanket to cover her modesty. The reaction to it was much like that produced by her later video 'Spinning Around': a lot of hormonally charged men gripped the side of their armchairs and prayed that they could be reincarnated as a favourite item in Kylie's wardrobe. 'As I get older,' Clive James, the Australian cultural commentator wistfully remarked, 'Kylie seems to be taking her clothes off at approximately twice the speed I'm putting mine on.'

But a backlash was beginning. Men of a certain age might be drooling over Kylie, but the rest of the world was taking a different point of view. Virgin Radio ran an ad campaign at the time: 'We've done something to improve Kylie's records,' it ran. 'We've banned them.' Even Pete Waterman was having reservations about the route chosen by his former protégée. 'Kylie changed,' he observed. 'She constantly wanted to be different – she wanted to deny what she was and is. I don't believe you have a right to do that to people who helped make you a millionaire. It's naughty. You can change but you can't tell people who really liked you that your old records were rubbish. Kylie might not know where she is at the moment and she may want to be somebody else but to a lot of people she's still Charlene from *Neighbours*.

'We can shift our image but no one can completely metamorphose like Kylie is trying to do,' he added. 'You are who you are. Oasis are superstars because they present themselves as they always were – boys from Manchester who scowl a lot and say foul-mouthed things. Björk's the same, but she's not putting it on. Kylie might want to be like Björk, but she can't – for a start Björk didn't come out singing "I Should Be So Lucky".' In retrospect, of course, Waterman was spot on. IndieKylie was never really convincing and it was only when Kylie returned to her pop roots that she again achieved the kind of success she had known in her early days. But everyone's allowed to make a few mistakes. This was Kylie's time.

One man was lucky enough to share Kylie's favours, temporarily, at least. At the beginning of 1995, after a gap of nearly two years, she embarked on her next proper relationship, with the model Mark Gerber, who was then 35. Kylie had seen him cavorting around naked in the film *Sirens*; as an onlooker at the time rather indelicately put it, 'Gerber had been a massive hit in the film and was clearly massively endowed, too. Kylie made him her mission.'

It was a mission in which she intended to succeed. Kylie asked him out on a date to cruise Sydney Harbour; by the end of it he was reportedly besotted. His parents were not so happy. 'Gerber was no spring chicken yet his parents were worried,' said a friend. As it turned out, the relationship didn't last very long anyway. 'It's in the past now,' says Gerber today. 'You move on.'

All the while, her search to be taken seriously continued. Kylie was popping up here, there and everywhere: judging the Look Of The Year model competition with Karen Mulder and Vivienne Westwood, lip-synching to a castrato for the mega-trendy artist Sam Taylor-Wood and appearing in the T in the Park rock festival at Hamilton's Strathclyde Country Park.

The latter marked her first-ever appearance at a British music festival and her fans were beside themselves with joy. 'She was unbelievable,' said Charlie Gibson from Glasgow. 'Better than I ever thought she would be.' And not forgetting her gay fans, Kylie managed to fit in a skimpily clad appearance at the Astoria Club during London's Gay Pride Festival, during which one woman managed to leap on stage and give her a kiss. 'Kylie looked tickled pink,' said an onlooker. 'She seemed to have forgotten to put on her dress and the crowd were going completely bonkers.'

Next Kylie really began to make waves, both in her choice of lover and duettist. The lover was comedian Pauly Shore, best known for his role in *California Man,* with whom she had a brief relationship that August. News that they were an item caused ructions, both because of Shore's wild man reputation and because his previous girlfriend had been a porn queen called Savannah, who had committed suicide the previous year. Kylie met Shore in Los Angeles where she was again making a bid for screen stardom in the film *Bio Dome,* in which Pauly also starred; she was actually still seeing Mark at the time, but that came to an abrupt end.

'It's definitely over,' said a friend. 'He guessed it was coming because Kylie left him in London while she filmed *Bio Dome* and he noticed her calls were becoming infrequent. Then one night she rang him and told him things weren't working out.

Mark was very upset and now he'll be even more hurt at finding he was dumped for another guy.'

It might well have been her continued hankering after Michael that made Kylie able to offer Pauly help, but help she did and for a short time it was just what both of them needed. Savannah, whose real name had been Shannen Wilsey and who had also been out with Guns N' Roses singer Axl Rose, died just a year after US comic Sam Kinnison, who had been like a father figure to Pauly. Friends were amazed at his new choice of partner. 'Pauly's been around the block a lot more than Kylie,' said one. 'It's an unbelievable match because she's so wholesome and he's so crazy. [But] Kylie is helping him realise that life's not all sadness. He has tended to go for tarty women and loves them and leaves them. But he has a lot more respect for Kylie. He's really smitten. He calls her lots of soppy names and is very gentle.'

Indeed, their brief relationship was really rather touching. 'At first, she just thought he was this crazy guy who made her laugh a lot,' said an insider who watched the relationship develop. 'But she started feeling something for him after he arranged a surprise birthday party for her on the set of *Bio Dome*. She'd flown her mom and dad from Australia because she thought her twenty-seventh birthday was going to be a lonely affair. But Pauly surprised them by wheeling out a big cake with the words Happy Birthday Barbie On The Shrimp. That's his nickname for her because she reminds him of a Barbie doll.' For her part, Kylie was realistic about her new man. 'While I don't know how long this will last with Pauly, I'm having fun again,' she said.

The relationship was not to last. And of *Bio Dome* – a would-be comedy about brothers who gatecrash a scientific experiment, which finally came out in 1996 – Kylie said this:

'You know with parents, you can do something not so great and they'll tell you they loved it? My dad said, "I can't believe you did that. That was just diabolical!" So I never watched it.' Kylie's character in the film, incidentally, was called Petra Von Kant, which might well have acted as a warning from the start ...

Next, Kylie managed to cause a really serious stir. She sang a duet with Nick Cave, an ex-heroin addict and Serious Artist who achieved the seemingly impossible and actually made her look unattractive in the video they recorded together. 'Where The Wild Roses Grow', a cheery little ditty about the murder of a woman called Eliza Day, reached number 11 in the charts – a reasonable performance from Kylie's point of view, but not outstanding; by contrast, it was Nick's most popular song to date. The single brought Kylie much credibility, but if you're in one of those moods where a glass of champagne and a quick burst of PopKylie is needed to cheer you up, this particular song is probably best avoided. It was written by Nick especially for Kylie. 'I wrote the song because I have the utmost respect for her,' he revealed. 'It's a song about a man who can't control his love for a girl, who finds her so beautiful he feels compelled to kill her.'

Label deConstruction was pleased to see Kylie's changing image. "Kylie is constantly reinventing herself and this is just another stage,' said a company spokesman. 'She is moving towards a heavier sound and working with Nick Cave is all part of that change.' Mercifully the stage didn't last long: Kylie spent most of the video lying in a river, à la Ophelia, sporting a seriously unwise red bobbed haircut and entertaining the attentions of Nick Cave, a rabbit, a millipede and a snake.

Kylie gave and still gives every indication of being star-struck by Nick, in a way that she's never been about anyone else. She has spoken wonderingly on a number of occasions about the fact that around the time she was singing 'I Should Be So Lucky', Nick was recovering from heroin addiction, the clear implication being that while Kylie was acting in a silly and frivolous way, Nick was experiencing life in the raw. 'I really didn't know that much about Nick Cave before I worked with him,' she admitted in *The Kylie Videodrome*, which came out in 2001. 'He contacted me about duetting with him on *Murder Ballads* [Nick's album of the time] and explained to me that for six years before that he had been thinking about recording with me but had waited. It is a mark of him and how he does things that he waited and waited until the time was right.'

Kylie was clearly incredibly impressed to be contacted by someone with a reputation like Nick Cave's. 'What is really special to me is that when he first thought about it, it was at the time when the most uncool thing you could say you wanted to do was to record a duet with Kylie Minogue,' she reflected. 'He thinks differently. He has amazing integrity and working with him was one of the best experiences I have ever had in my career.'

Making the video – and it must be said, Kylie is a trouper when it comes to her videos – was to prove a slightly less than pleasant experience, especially when it came to her co-stars. 'There was mention of a snake – I didn't really think too much about that,' she said. 'We'd done a few takes of this and that and I was sitting in the chair and I noticed the director and the assistant director just speaking with each other but looking quite suspicious. And I look over and see what is going on. Then the animal handler joins them and the snake joins them and I think: 'OK, it's the snake time.'

'I had never handled, touched, held a snake before so I am probably sounding very typical to the snake handler of someone who is about to get up close and personal to a snake for the first time ... The snake was a star in that video but there was also Hermann the millipede, who I believe has been on a number of videos. These guys were telling me, "This is Hermann the millipede and he has been on so and so and so and so." So between Hermann, the snake and the bunny rabbit you notice me as well somehow.'

For some people, at least, it was a mercy to have something to take your mind off the song itself. 'Although a good track musically,' said one critic, 'the lyrics are quite depressing.' As an understatement that ranks alongside: 'It's a little bit hot in the Sahara' and fortunately for the sanity of the nation, Kylie was soon camping it up again with the undisputed Queen of Kitsch, Sir Elton John. The couple sang a duet together, 'Sisters', at the Equality 95 event at the Royal Albert Hall organised by gay rights pressure group Stonewall: Kylie sported a minuscule little tassly number while Sir Elt came on stage replete in black evening dress, long black satin gloves and blond wig. The duet was a great success.

'When I decided to dress in a frock for the Stonewall show, I wanted to sing "Sisters", an old song from my youth,' Elton wrote in Kylie's 1999 book *Kylie*. 'However, I needed someone to sing it with. Kylie immediately sprung to mind as she would get the spirit of the idea. It turned out so well – not only was she completely rehearsed and note perfect, she was so much fun and a dream to perform with. As I'd always been a huge fan (since *Neighbours*!) I was extremely impressed. I'm not easily impressed! Simply, she is divine – multi-talented.'

Sir Elt was not the only person who thought that. By this time Kylie was going out with the French photographer

Stephane Sednaoui, with whom she'd driven across America after making *Bio Dome*; she fell for him when he picked her up and held her above his head at a party. Stephane was 34 to Kylie's 29 and he was to become her second great love (or third, if you count Jason): 'We were stuck together in a car for three weeks and we really bonded,' said an exuberant Kylie. 'We're in love.'

A couple of years previously it would have seemed an unlikely coupling but at the time Stephane seemed the ideal companion for the new IndieKylie. Formerly engaged to the eccentric Icelandic singer Björk, Stephane had made videos for Madonna, U2, Tina Turner and Alanis Morisette and had a reputation for unusual behaviour (sex in public places) and an unusual appearance (a mohican haircut). For the first time since Michael, Kylie had met a man she felt she could truly look up to: the rest of the world was rather concerned, though, as Kylie appeared to wither away under their very eyes.

Never exactly overweight at the best of times, Kylie shrank to a shadow of her former self; there were reports, always denied, that she wasn't eating properly. She and Stephane were spotted in restaurants in which Kylie did little more than toy with a lettuce leaf. She seemed pale and tired, with bags under her eyes and a tired quality to her skin. And not only did she appear to have lost weight, but she embraced grunge with a vengeance, regularly appearing in public in baggy trousers and trainers, sporting a cropped haircut and wearing no make-up. To put it bluntly, the woman looked rough.

For fans of SexKylie, it was all a bit much. In no time rumours started circulating that Kylie was anorexic or, worse still, on drugs: Kylie laughed it all off and promptly disrobed for a photo session with *i-D* magazine. 'Kylie is NOT anorexic,' insisted a spokesman. 'She has never been healthier or happier. She almost died laughing when she read the anorexia story. Kylie thinks these photos prove that far from being ill, she is at her healthiest.' Kylie was certainly playing it up for all she was worth: she informed the magazine that she only wore clothes when necessary and was at her happiest being naked with Stephane. And who would she personally like to undress? 'Him, him!' she cried in response.

The couple spent a great deal of time in Paris, where Kylie had bought a flat. As to what she was like when she was in love, Kylie admitted, 'I'm pretty helpless, actually, uncontrollable. My manager hates it when I'm in love. Being in love is the coolest thing in the world. The coolest and the cruellest.'

But as with Kylie's other relationships, it was not to last. Kylie and Stephane stayed together for two years. After the split, Stephane fell in love with the model Laetitia Casta, who went on to bear his child. Kylie seemed singularly unmoved by the parting of the ways. 'I want this on the record: I'm not grieving,' she said firmly, in an interview given just a couple of days after they broke up. 'I wouldn't be wearing make-up if we were still together. [That in itself, considering that she is one of the world's most glamorous women, might be an indication as to what had gone wrong.] This relationship lasted two years and Stephane and I had some great times. People grow in different directions sometimes, don't they? It's mutual. Everything's great. I'm not a hard woman, but I'm not too bad over this one.'

Some clue as to why they broke up came some years later in an interview Kylie gave. Although she did not specify which boyfriend she was talking about, she referred to being suffocated by an older man. 'I won't say who,' she said. 'But it's something I had to go through to recognise it doesn't suit me. It sounds so horribly clichéd, but I need to be able to just flit around for a bit and come back. I'm childlike. I felt I had a box around me. It's like your colours fade and you're a much lesser version of yourself. And it's just not fair on you or anyone else. You're wilting. It's not good.'

Another clue came with the revelation that she had painted her flat. Until she moved to Shoreditch in 2002, Kylie lived in a large home in Chelsea, which was for a time completely white, with wooden floorboards, a large sofa and a kitchen bench. Flowers provided the colour. In 1997, Kylie remarked, 'You would never know it's my place. There's no indication of it being my place whatsoever.' After splitting from Stephane, all this changed. Kylie painted the front of the house red, the front rooms pistachio, the kitchen pink and the kitchen bench chocolate. 'My house had been white forever,' she said, 'when I broke up with Stephane – which was harmonious – I wanted colour. I was like, right. I broke through!'

It might well have been that Kylie was also beginning to look at her relationships with men – both on a professional and personal basis – in a new light. 'I'm not a complete doormat with men,' she said. 'I'm just grateful and proud to work with them. It's true I've never really worked with women. If it is true that men have had control over my career, then there is more balance coming – I'm taking control but I can't work alone. I need support around me.'

Of course, in a career like Kylie's, it is sensible to take advice and guidance from others in the business. But this seemed to have spilled into her personal life as well. 'I always end up being the pupil in the relationship,' she reflected, sounding as if she wasn't entirely delighted about that fact. 'I'm always the one asking the questions and being fascinated by the answers. Sometimes I feel I'm just in the way.

'I've looked very hard at why I end up in the relationships I do. I was always Daddy's girl. He's an accountant and he had always looked after my money and told me when I need to save and when it's okay to go crazy. He's clever and I respect him. But I am aware that men taking a lead may come from that. I never rebelled. I might have worn some odd clothes and smoked a cigarette, but I never rejected my parents and their lifestyle. My mum worked on my tour a couple of years ago in the wardrobe department – there's not many pop stars who would admit that. You're not supposed to be a pop star and have your parents helping out backstage, are you?'

No, you're not, but that never bothered Kylie. She was, however, going to need parental support and indeed all the support she could get throughout the next phase of her career, when pop's pixie princess became more indie than ever and seemingly went too far. For the first time ever, Kylie Minogue looked as if she might be facing the end of her career.

9

The Wilderness Years

Kylie Minogue was about to embark on one of the most difficult periods of her life. It was 1997 and she hadn't had an album out for three years. She was still out to achieve credibility, still battling demons from the past and still unsure as to where to go in the future. Again, it was Nick Cave who was responsible for her next inspired act – standing up at the Poetry Olympics in the Royal Albert Hall and reciting the lyrics to 'I Should Be So Lucky'.

It was actually Nick himself who was first invited to stand up and recite. 'He's so clever,' reminisces Kylie fondly. 'He just planted the seed so well. I wanted to go and see him perform and the day before he called me up and mentioned that it was an open affair and if I wanted to get up and do something I could. Thank you, I said, but don't think so, poetry, never done it before, uh-uh.'

Nick, however, was not to be put off that easily and so it was that the next night a disbelieving audience watched Kylie walk up on stage. 'Hi,' she began. 'I didn't expect to be here today but here I am and I'm going to recite something I didn't write. "In my imagination, there is no complication, I dream about you all the time..."' The crowd went wild.

It was a brave act for someone who felt embarrassed about her past. 'It was like I'd climbed Mount Everest or jumped out of a plane,' Kylie said afterwards. 'So many things that I had avoided for so long were right there. That was what Nick was saying to me: "It'll be brilliant, it'll confront your past, all in one fell swoop." And he was right.

'I am far more accepting about everything I did then. They carved out their own little niche in musical history and it blows my mind that I was part of it. For so long I had such an embarrassment about the early days ... I was running as fast as I could away from it but now I realise actually I was pretty cool.'

It also took some courage to appear as she did: the audience got a very rare sighting of ScruffKylie. 'I was wearing green tracksuit pants and a purple T-shirt, no make-up – it was the weekend and I was so scruffy. Until I'd got the first line out I was thinking, I'm not so sure about this... I broke so many rules. I didn't take any of the steps I would normally take before a live performance. I hadn't done any of the preparation, you know, slipping in to your "ego outfit", the mental thing. I remember I was watching it with Nick on a monitor backstage and the guy before me was this old white-haired man with a long beard, reading poetry in Braille, and I said, "Nick, God's on stage, how can we follow that?" But after he pushed me on and I read the first line – I had a friend scribble them out – I heard a titter run through the audience and I knew I had them. The reaction told me they knew what it was. I am still amazed that he thought of it, that I did it and by the effect it had on people and on me.'

And she was open about the effect Nick had had on her. 'I saw Nick last night and there is a great mutual respect which is incredible,' she said in an interview in 1997. 'If I stop to think about it I am baffled, because considering where I come from, I would just never have expected that I would end up in that situation.' So did she feel cool now? 'It depends. I feel happy. I feel very excited about the future and very accepting of the past.'

The immediate future, though, was to be very difficult. It was in 1997 that Michael Hutchence was found dead, hanging from the back of a hotel door in Sydney. Kylie was utterly devastated and appeared pale and wan at the funeral, although with typical generosity she spoke out in defence of Paula Yates, Michael's partner and the mother of his child, when she was criticised for making Michael's life problematic. 'The people who criticise her have taken no responsibility for their actions,' Kylie fumed. 'They make me very angry. Paula has a lot to deal with at the moment.'

And it was around the end of 1997 that she finally brought out a new album – which, in turn, eventually convinced Kylie that she had no need to worry about everyone taking her seriously and that it was absolutely fine to go back to boppy little disco numbers. She wasn't quite there yet, though, and so it was that she went through the worst period of her career – and all because of her second album for deConstruction.

Kylie wanted this album to work; it was to give her the status of being a serious artist that she so very much craved, not least because she had written a lot of it. 'It's my album more than ever before,' she said firmly. 'Although I am reluctant to make declarations because I've said so many things before and realised later they were only right for the time. But to this point, it is the album I've had the most to do with. There are 12 tracks and I've written all the lyrics, except one which was a co-write.'

Despite Kylie's enthusiasm, there were problems right from the outset. For a start, it had taken three years to get the album into the shops as Kylie continued to meet the grooviest people in the business, formulate all sorts of exciting plans and then come up with nothing that was particularly exciting. Not that it was her fault. She had made it plain right from the outset that she was counting on the creative powers that be at deConstruction to help her find interesting new projects and if they were not able to do so, then they really had no one but themselves to blame.

And the timing of the album could not have been worse. Originally entitled Impossible Princess, it was first due to be released in January 1997 as a collaboration between Kylie and the Brothers in Rhythm. At the last minute, though, it was decided that more collaborators were needed and so the Manic Street Preachers, Dave Ball from The Grid and a host of others were drafted in to turn Kylie into the ultimate indie impossible princess.

The next release date was set to be September 1997, which turned out to be just a couple of weeks after Princess Diana was killed in a car crash. Both the release date and the title were immediately put on hold: it would have been massively inappropriate (and commercial suicide) to have done anything else. 'I've lived with that title for two years,' said Kylie sombrely, explaining the changes and her own reaction to Diana's death. 'And I had already done a lot of press talking about the name, but after the tragedy of Princess Di occurred, we had to rethink.

'It didn't hit me immediately, because I found it so hard to comprehend. But then I thought I don't want to be constantly explaining or upsetting people. So we've taken the name off for now, but I'd like to keep the option for putting it back in the future. That's what the album is called, it just won't be on the cover.' And guess who was responsible for the title? 'It came from a book of poetry, *Poems To Break The Hearts Of Impossible Princesses*, by the poet Billy Childish who gave it to Nick to give to me,' Kylie explained earnestly. Truly, Nick Cave has a lot to feel responsible for ...

Kylie loved the name, though. 'The first time I saw *Impossible Princess* on the Billy Childish book, it had my name written all over it,' she gushed, having perhaps mislaid the spectacles she'd sported on the cover of her previous album. 'I can be the girl on the show pony at the circus with sparkles and sequins and I adore the spotlight – so that's her [the Impossible Princess]. And then there's the flip side of me, which is completely not that ... the green tracksuit pants ... no make-up and being a wreck! I regard it [the title] with humour, with irony and with a certain amount of realism because I can change my mind about things all the time and be completely impossible.

'It is about practically everything, even impossible things – the desire to have all my senses fulfilled, to experience life in the broadest possible way ... I'd like to think that if you make yourself open to almost anything, then those experiences will come ... I talk about it and hope to do it at some point.'

At first, Kylie thought that her change of image would go down well. 'People love to pigeonhole you, no matter what you do,' she argued. 'They place a box over you and you can't get out of it, but I have been able to stretch it a little each way, to lift up one side and peep out, to shuffle it here and there. I know that's not normal. I don't know how I've done it. I was supposed to be a one-hit wonder. I can remember having my second hit and thinking, mmmmm ...'

In many ways, Kylie was right: she had been able to change

her image, although given that she went from girl next door to sex bomb – as opposed to say, going from sex bomb to middle-aged housewife – her continuing popularity was perhaps not such a surprise. And she had shown courage: it's hard to imagine, for example, Victoria Beckham going on stage in a poetry recital at the Royal Albert Hall and reciting the lyrics to 'Wannabe' (although it's very easy to envisage Madonna taking on such a challenge with one of her own songs). But with the benefit of hindsight, it's clear that Kylie's new persona didn't work because it simply wasn't her: she's appeared much happier in recent years as born-again SexKylie than she ever looked drowning in a river with a rose over her face. Actually, to be fair, she adored her collaboration with Nick Cave – it's what came next that was to prove the real problem.

But back to the album. This was Kylie's indie moment and she was bubbling over with enthusiasm. 'It's eclectic, some dance, some guitar-based pop,' she burbled happily. 'One track is a smoky nightclub thing, another is psychedelic and one of them is almost reggae. I'm reluctant to say it's all personal because it sounds like gush, but they all came from moments, little vignettes, different stories. It was about going inwards, it wasn't like I was looking for stories. I always had a pad and pen with me and the lyrics I'm most pleased with came out whole. They just said everything I wanted to say. I just had my head down trying to do something that was truthful to myself. I'm pleased with it, but I'm much more pleased it's out. I felt overly pregnant because it's been two years in the making. Now it's out, I can fully let go of it. But it's scary, because if it doesn't work, I can't blame anyone else.'

Those words were to be prophetic, as were Kylie's next thoughts on the matter. 'I have become a symbol of having things too easy,' she admitted. 'But I don't take it for granted. I admit I have a great life. I have a great family and a job I enjoy. I don't have to turn up to a job I hate every day. I know I'm lucky.'

The album, not very imaginatively retitled *Kylie Minogue*, came out in early 1998. Despite her brave words, Kylie might have had an inkling that there would be problems, for by this time she was only too eager to dismiss the idea that she was after anything as trivial as a number one. After all, she'd been there, done that and bought the hot pants. 'I've had to redefine success for my sanity,' she said in an interview at the time, 'because if I put the expectation of massive success, which I had in the past, on myself to try and maintain all those chart positions which I had initially, I'd go round the bend. You know, number one, number two, number one, number two, they were all top 10. I'm not expecting that. Musical fashion is constantly changing and if Gina [G] is the fashion now like I used to be it doesn't worry me. What a diabolical state that world would be if those changes didn't take place.'

They were noble sentiments, well expressed, but not the type guaranteed to bring a smile to the lips of her record company. Kylie, however, was still giving every impression of being blissfully happy with the way the album had gone, not least because she was involved in writing the lyrics, something that had long been her ambition. 'They're all autobiographical,' she revealed. 'They're all what I've felt, been through ... I don't know how to write any other way. Even if I did I wouldn't want to. I haven't reached the stage yet where if the songs aren't smash hits I'm going to take it personally. I don't have extra nerves about the fact that I've written this album. I've got the same nerves and excitement as I have with every album. It's, "Please do okay."'

And Nick Cave was still playing as big a part in Kylie's life as ever. 'What I was going to say about redefining success is that the one and only Nick Cave, who I totally adore these days ... I did a performance with him in October. He called up and asked whether I was interested in doing a song in a jazz café the next day in London. He said it was a song he'd just written three days prior and modestly he said, "I think it's really good and I know it's late notice but would you do it."

'And so the next day I found myself at another poetry-type affair which was much smaller [than the Poetry Olympics at the Royal Albert Hall] singing this gorgeous ... piece with Nick Cave and I realised then that if I had the opportunity of a number one record or doing this with Nick Cave, I'd probably choose doing this with Nick because that's something, a moment, that's just fantastic: a miserable, grey rainy Saturday afternoon in London and we were in such a tiny environment.'

Kylie continued her praise of Nick, becoming slightly incoherent in her excitement. 'I wasn't nervous when I first met Nick because I hate to admit that I was really naïve and didn't know about this god that was Nick Cave, the icon,' she gushed. 'That's probably part of the reason he'd been wanting to do something with me for a while; I'm so far removed from where he comes from that in a strange way it makes our meeting more harmonious ... to come from the Birthday Party [Nick's first band] and me trying to speed-read his autobiography and learning about urination at various gigs and whacking the people over the heads with microphones ... to meet when you've got all that space between [us], for [us] to overcome, to get to that point, I just think it's gorgeous and it constantly thrills me.'

Nick more than returned the compliment: for a start, his

name was romantically linked with Kylie's. Kylie is incredibly good at turning down men she's not interested in and still making them feel like heroes – Robbie Williams, a couple of years later, was a case in point – and the full Minogue charm came into play in Nick's case too. So Nick had the hots for her? 'Umm,' mused Kylie. 'I do know he was talking about that. He would say to me around that time, "I've been talking about you again and all my stories keep getting more and more exaggerated and obsessive." I think he knows that I'm slightly in love with him and if the feeling's mutual, then that's nice. He's had such an impact on my life. He's lovely and gorgeous and intelligent.' In the middle of all of this it's quite easy to miss the fact that their relationship never actually progressed – rather, you suspect, to Nick's chagrin – beyond friendship and artistic collaboration.

Kylie did, however, become some sort of muse, to the extent that she inspired a Cave lecture entitled *The Secret Life Of The Love Song*. Originally conceived for the Vienna Poetry Festival, it was a reflection on Nick's artistic muse and the whole genre of love songs, and was eventually delivered to a capacity audience – and great acclaim – at the Royal Festival Hall.

Kylie might have been more credible than at any other time in her career, but, sadly, she was also a good deal less popular than she had ever been before. The record-buying public simply didn't want GrungeKylie. It was SexKylie who was the stuff both of adolescent and middle-aged male fantasy, to say nothing of a role model for her female fans. And so nothing went according to plan. The single 'Some Kind Of Bliss' was released in September: it spent one week in the charts at number 22. Its follow-up, 'Did It Again', got to number 14, as did the next one, 'Breathe'. The album, when it was finally released, made it to number 10.

To be fair, the timing was seriously out. 'Some Kind Of Bliss' was released in the same week as 'Candle In The Wind '97', Sir Elton John's ballad to the late Princess of Wales. It didn't stand a chance. 'I think the statistic was that Elton had 75 per cent of the singles bought that week, so mine didn't get off to a good start,' admitted Kylie a couple of months after the single had been released. 'I've told myself not to be frustrated but actually I am frustrated, because the album should be out. The point of it is to get it out and maybe people will like it, maybe they'll love it, maybe they'll hate it. But at least it will be out of my hands. I could be upset about it but then you look at the bigger picture and I have no right to be annoyed. It's just been delayed because a tragedy occurred. Being born under a lucky star, I'm used to seeing things go smooth. It was a reality check. Shit happens.'

With such problems with her current pop career, Kylie was now beginning to appreciate her former mentors rather more. For some time she had been resentful of the fact that Stock, Aitken and Waterman had pretty much run her career with little input from the star herself, but she was beginning to understand that there was something to be said for working with a team who got you to the top of the charts on a pretty regular basis. This dawning realisation came when Kylie was accosted on the street one day.

'I bumped in to Mrs Stock the other day,' she said in the same interview. 'She came up to me and said, "I'm Mike Stock's wife." Now I don't know what those guys are up to now but I said to her, "Please say hello." There was a period when I wasn't speaking very highly of them, but time changes a lot of things. For whatever we've been through, there's a lot to look back on and a lot to be pleased with.'

As time wore on, the records continued not to sell well and

'Is this the end?' headlines started appearing. GrungeKylie vanished almost overnight, while SexKylie suddenly started making a reappearance. Kylie began explaining earnestly that, actually, grunge wasn't quite her. 'I can only say that I do what comes naturally to me and I think it would be more of a lie for me to be wearing baggy pants and be coy and demure and not giving a nod to my sexuality,' she said. 'I've tried to tone down my flirtatiousness but it's not something I think I should be ashamed of,' she went on. 'I don't think it's cheap in any way, I hope people can see I'm having fun with it.'

But still nothing seemed to be going right. For a while Kylie appeared to be in danger of being eclipsed by her fellow Australian Natalie Imbruglia, who also starred in *Neighbours*, and who was now also pursuing a singing career: when *Breathe* was released, music paper *NME* rather loftily pronounced, 'Kylie now sounds exactly like Natalie.'

Kylie fought back. She emphasised the fact that she was now entirely at ease with her past. 'So many people have stories that relate to my career,' she said. 'I heard about an obsessed fan who'd got a cardboard cut-out of me and his girlfriend asked him to turn it around when they made love. You hear them just sitting in cabs talking to the driver or just talking to people in the street. They just spill out and then the tellers are kind of embarrassed. I just say, "Okay, it's funny."'

And still the records did badly. Finally, by August 1998 everyone, Kylie included, had had enough. 'Kylie and deConstruction recently reached an amicable agreement not to do another album together,' read a statement released by the record company. 'She has been freed from any further contractual obligations.' In actual fact there was nothing amicable about it: the album had sold only 43,000, not even in the same league as her first album, *Kylie*, which had sold two million copies a decade earlier. Things were getting difficult behind the scenes: there were reports that in June record company bosses had told her, 'If sales don't take off, we'll dump you.'

And when the moment came, her new colleagues weren't much more positive off the record. 'Kylie has tried nearly every kind of music style and image change, so there really wasn't anywhere else for her to go,' said a deConstruction insider. 'The company felt they had stuck with her for a long time but ultimately she wasn't going to recapture her earlier success.'

It was a tremendous slap in the face for Kylie. As it happened, the 'Kylie dumped' headlines were not telling the whole story, given that she was by this time absolutely desperate to leave deConstruction, but it was a public humiliation none the less. It was deConstruction that scored a coup in getting Kylie, not the other way round, and now it was as if she was being publicly branded a has-been. It was a very uncomfortable moment in what had been an incredibly successful career.

'I was losing them money and I wasn't having any joy,' she says in retrospect. 'I wasn't at the meeting [where it was decided the label would drop her] but they wanted to let me go and I would have asked to go. It was blatantly obvious that it wasn't working. It wasn't like one dumped the other and the other wanted it to stay the same. I actually thought it was the best thing.' She was asked if she had bad days – and, indeed, if she could have retired. 'Like, "I have no qualifications, what am I going to do?"' she asked rhetorically. 'No, I didn't wallow in depression … I don't think I could retire and have the life that I'm accustomed to. Not that I have fabulous Elton John expenses, but things like getting on a plane and getting a first-class ticket …'

At least one fellow musician managed to find a bit of humour in the situation, as well as offering some unqualified support for the diminutive pop star. 'Kylie, love her to bits,' said James Dean Bradfield of the Manic Street Preachers, with whom Kylie had appeared on stage in Shepherd's Bush. 'I'm her number one fan. She's so tiny and gorgeous. I could eat her. She got dropped by her label after working with me, which I'm eternally sorry for.'

And so, just like the rest of us, Kylie needed to work out how to earn money and needed to rewrite her plans. She chose the most sensible course of action available: she had a fundamental rethink about what she wanted to do next and what had gone wrong in recent years. 'I don't think it was a mistake,' says Kylie now with commendable honesty. 'I think it was ... I wanted more help than I had then.

'In retrospect, looking back at a lot of the lyrics, it's quite obvious now that I was saying, "Erm, hello? Yes, I am drowning, not waving, can I have a bit of help here?" It was a period where things weren't gelling together for lots of reasons. But I don't think it was a mistake and I don't regret it because I learned a lot during that period.' She certainly did. She learned that disco is her natural home, that men prefer her in hot pants to tracksuits – and, above all, that when you have had a severe setback, it is crucial to get on your feet and start all over again.

'So many people said to me, "Don't give yourself a hard time,"' she recalled later. 'It wasn't successful, not a commercial success, but they really liked it and they thought it showed a side of me that won't come across in an interview, or a TV show, or a video. That it's probably more enlightening than anybody realised at the time. It was an experience ... it was a long one. It took two years to make that album and then it just seemed like there was bad luck around it.' It's worth noting here that Kylie puts a great deal of emphasis on luck: unlike less modest stars, she has always emphasised that luck played a big part in her career. She also recognises that on the whole, she has had a lot of it.

'It was due for release,' she went on, 'then it wasn't released, then it came out with a different title, which was the same title of an old record ... it left me having to do a lot of work by myself, and I didn't really know where I was going or what I was doing. But I think that brought out something different and interesting because it hadn't been heard before.'

At least Australia still loved its most famous daughter. In 1998, the Australian government gave her an achievement award for her contribution to Australia's export industry, while a picture of her signed in pink lipstick hangs as one of the centrepieces at Australia's National Portrait Gallery in Canberra. That is not the only Kylie-related exhibit in Australia's museums, incidentally – the wedding dress she wore as Charlene Robinson is on permanent display at the Melbourne Museum. Having come to something of a crisis point in her career, Kylie did what daughters the world over do when they're having a miserable time – she went home.

Home in this case meant a tour of Australia, following a tour of Britain, and it was exactly what Kylie needed. Titled 'Intimate and Live', the tour was a sell-out in both Britain and Australia, but it was while performing in the second of those two countries that Kylie really began to find her musical feet again as she revisited many of her old hits, even including 'Locomotion'. She camped it up, she went back to glitz and the fans loved her for it. 'I made a conscious decision just to be myself,' she said. 'That's why some of it couldn't be camper. Showy. Pretty much the way I am.' She was delighted when fans approached her and told her they used to wear Kylie earrings. 'It was amazing meeting a lot of people who said, "I've grown up with you"', she enthused. 'That's beautiful. I don't mean to sound cosmic, but I love the fact I've had a moment with all these people.'

The *Herald Sun*, Australia's biggest selling daily newspaper, reflected the mood of the crowd at each of the 24 dates:

For a concert where she could do no wrong, Kylie Minogue did everything right at the Palais theatre last night. The 'seven-minute crowd' she called the audience of more than 2,000 fans, referring to how long it took to sell the tickets. She may not have had to prove herself but she put on an event and not a gig. Opening with the intense 'Too Far', Minogue instantly vindicated her choice of bands (John Farnham Band) with imported percussionist and guitarist, easily replicating the musical boundary-pushing on her albums. Minogue used the concert, her first in seven years, to re-write her past. Her Stock/Aitken/ Waterman songs were reinvented, a gospel rock 'What Do I Have To Do', a Las Vegas cabaret for '…Lucky'. From rock grooves some kind of bliss through to a seriously camp cover of 'Dancing Queen', Minogue left no musical stone unturned. The recent hit 'Did It Again' thrilled the crowd, as did the hard-edged 'Limbo.' The encore featured her classic 'Confide In Me', with the show closing with a re-worked version of 'Better The Devil You Know'. Minogue thanked the crowd for her homecoming before leaving the stage. A Star Is Reborn.

It was a bonus that *Impossible Princess* had actually sold well in Australia – it was released on time, kept its original title and eventually became a platinum seller there – but Kylie had realised that what her audience wanted from her was pop. 'When I was doing the concerts in Australia, I made the decision, way back then, to get back in to pop,' says Kylie. 'I guess I was testing it out. I'd just do what I do but if it came across as daggy, then I'd just go for it. Everything I've done has always been pop. It's just been in different guises. It has changed according to where I was in my life.'

Kylie had finally realised where her strengths lay: in glamour and froth. 'I never thought I'd fucked it up completely,' she says today. 'But I wasn't following my instinct. I wasn't being as true to myself as I should be. I lost my way.'

While in Australia, Kylie made the film *Sample People*, which was yet another to forget about afterwards – 'although visually *Sample People* remains a pleasure, the plot, story and lack of character development let it down,' wrote one critic. Perhaps the best way to explain what was wrong with the film is to quote *Australian Cosmopolitan*: 'The film's a kind of Aussie *Pulp Fiction*. Kylie plays a drug snorting gangster's moll and Ben's [Mendelsohn, her co-star, whom she had first met in *The Henderson Kids*] a bitchy bisexual.' It was, according to the same magazine, 'Kylie's attempt to establish herself as a happening, indie movie star.'

The film went the way of all of Kylie's other indie attempts, but otherwise all was well. She was in Australia, with her people. And she was with a record company who appreciated her, too: Mushroom Records, the label she has been with in Australia throughout her entire career. Towards the end of the year, Kylie played at the Concert

Of The Century at Melbourne Cricket ground to celebrate Mushroom's twenty-fifth anniversary: the crowds went wild and Kylie cheered up. She was ready to take on the world again.

10

The Divine Miss M

B ack in Britain, the first real sign of a reawakening of interest in Kylie was a coffee-table book, packed choc-full of pictures of the petite diva herself. Kylie had been considering doing a book from as early as 1992, but when it finally appeared, it was different both from Madonna's *Sex*, a volume of extreme exhibitionism, and Kylie's own initial idea. There are a couple of nude photographs to delight Kylie-watchers, but on the whole, the book is really a scrapbook of Kylie's career to date.

These are pictures of Kylie stemming right back to the earliest days, tracking her career from TV tomboy to sex kitten, with the pages devoted to Kylie lookalikes, paintings of Kylie, Kylie's face drawn on a man's leg, Kylie and Michael, photographs by Stephane, an abstract painting by Jason Donovan, magazine covers, record covers and so on. Kylie was at last coming to terms with her sugar sweet past. She was also, not a moment too soon, growing out of her IndieKylie phase. ComebackKylie was on her way.

'It was born out of a moment of boredom,' says the woman

herself. 'I was sat in my kitchen with a friend, having just finished the best tour I've ever done and I was in need of a project to get me through the lull.' The lull, of course, was Kylie's period between record labels, a period that was clearly being put to extremely creative use.

The book, called *Kylie*, is a collaboration between Kylie and her long-term stylist Will Baker in which she adopts all sorts of different persona – as indeed she has done throughout her career – and it is finished off with comments on Kylie by people ranging from Nick Cave to Julie Burchill. Nick Cave, incidentally, spends most of his entry ruminating on the words to 'Better The Devil You Know'. The first picture in the book is a little bit startling: Kylie having not so much a bad hair day as a bad all over day, right down to a smudge of lipstick on her lips. Her complexion is waxen, her eyes rigid and she just doesn't come across as bouncy little Kylie we all know and love. It is only when you look again that you realise this is actually a photograph of a waxwork of Kylie, rather than the woman herself.

'I made a bit of a blunder there,' admits Kylie chirpily. 'I just assumed people would go, "Oh, the waxwork", but they don't … It's funny when I'm with them because they just don't know what to say. I have to pounce on them and go, "Er … that's wax, darling!"'

There are a couple of pictures of a completely naked Kylie, one rather enchanting one taken in her dressing room after a concert. 'The reason I included that shot was because I remember the moment it was taken and I was so happy,' she says. 'But it's not there to shock, it's tasteful. Sure, nobody's ever seen my nipple before, but it means nothing to me. It's a nipple. Big deal.'

Kylie was aware that the book could be judged as vanity

publishing but was keen also to portray her new project as an assessment of her career to date. 'There is a certain amount of vanity involved,' she admits, 'but, as I say in the book, something of celebrity is self-centredness, the rest is insecurity.' And does she like the pictures of herself? 'Generally yes, but I keep it all in perspective,' she says.

'I know that anyone could look good if they had the same amount of help that I have. I've got the luxury of being able to change on a whim. I'm like the eight-year-old with the dress-up box. But I still get away with it! I change characters when I do a photo shoot. It's kind of avoiding being me – which I've become very good at. It's hard for me to explain, but rather than being captured, I become a new character or I choose a facet of me and let [it] take over.'

Given the number of different poses she strikes and the compilation of images from her past, the book can also be seen as some sort of search for the real Kylie Minogue. Is she IndieKylie, SexKylie, Charlene, ComebackKylie, SophisticatKylie – just what really constitutes the identity of the sweet little songstress from Oz? 'I tried to understand it with the book that I did,' she admitted a year after it had come out, 'but I think it confused me even more.'

The project was an ideal diversion from Kylie's recent problems and also one that suited her personality very well. 'I have a very low boredom threshold,' she says. 'It's a thread that runs through every aspect of my life and career.' And this did not just apply to work. 'When I go out with different men, I take on board certain aspects of their characters. I think we all do that, don't we?'

The magazine *Loaded* felt that Kylie's move into books was a very good move indeed. It even felt moved to publish a little review, which it put alongside two revealing pictures of Kylie:

Aussie popster's saucy book. Have a word – it's Kylie in a radical departure from Planet Pop. Yep, the diminutive Antipodean saucepot is back after a break from the charts, with her new book, Kylie. Packed with pics not unlike these two, it's supposed to challenge our view of the UK's favourite Sheila. Looks like she's going about it the right way and no mistake. This is a bold move into print, Kyles.

By this time, even through the bad patch, Kylie had been famous for a very long time and she was clearly beginning to reassess her past and look towards what she would be doing in the future. Unlike so many artists, though, who crave fame and then find it destroys them, Kylie has actually been able to take a step back and ponder what makes an audience so interested in the person up there on stage. 'The closest I can get to understanding it is if I'm sitting at the dentist and there's a magazine. I will pick it up and work my way through it and find myself saying, "Are they going out together? Look what she's wearing!" We all like a bit of gossip. It's like looking into people's houses when it's night-time and you can see inside. I like that. "Ooooh, look how they've decorated."'

Kylie was also aware of the fact that people liked putting her into specific persona, as witnessed by the pictures in the book. 'I think everyone's got a different version either that they want me to be or they imagine me to be,' she said. 'But I think there is a very human element to the relationship that my audience and myself have in that I can't double-cross them. I don't get away with things when it's not really me or when I make mistakes they kind of go, "Oh, she's going through a phase, she'll come to her senses."' The lessons of the recent past were clearly ringing very loudly in her ears.

Meanwhile, her love life was perking up again. There had

been no one serious since she split up with Stephane Sednaoui in 1997, but towards the end of 1998 Kylie followed in the footsteps of many another pretty girl in London (or so it sometimes seems) and had a fling with Tim Jefferies, the erstwhile companion of Koo Stark, Elle Macpherson and others too numerous to mention. It was only to last for three months, but it contributed to Kylie once again feeling at one with the world.

'Tim's gorgeous,' she says. 'He's funny and good looking. I'd known him for several years as a friend. In fact, he's the only friend I've ever dated and we've stayed friends. But in between the friendships it was definitely a romance. Elton John lent us his villa in the South of France for a romantic weekend. It's an amazing place with fantastic art – every room's immaculate. My life's rarely like that. I don't hang out with the Euro crowd – in fact, I haven't really met any of them. My friends are all unknown creative types who are nutters.'

They weren't all completely unknown – for example, Nick Cave – but in that way, at least, IndieKylie had been a success. She had found the people she wanted to hang out with. Even now she still spends time with the art crowd and the alternative brigade – one friend is Steve Strange, the Eighties pop star who recently published his autobiography, *Blitzed*! In the book, he recalls a joint birthday party he shared with Kylie. The guests found the old club/fashion and crossover brigade – George Michael, Zandra Rhodes, Duggie Fields and Andrew Logan – and Strange's 'new crowd' – promoter Lawrence Malice, Lisa B, Robert Hanson, Jason Donovan.

Back with Tim Jefferies, Kylie was having a great time. In time-honoured fashion, the couple were snapped together on a topless beach while they were on holiday in the South of France and they even managed to remain together for a few months afterwards before the affair fizzled out. Both were pictured with other people; Tim ended up, albeit briefly, with the statuesque German model Claudia Schiffer. His father Richard had this to say about his son's activities: 'I would have stuck with Kylie. I think Kylie's hot and I would like to give her one. But to go from that to this big silly fräulein ...' Perhaps unsurprisingly, given that little outburst, Tim and his father are estranged.

Had she wanted to, Kylie had the chance to swap notes with another of Tim's exes, Elle Macpherson, when the two appeared on the cover of *Australian Vogue* in September 1999. It takes something to be able to hold your own against one of the world's greatest supermodels, especially when she's about a foot taller than you – the interviewer describes the two embracing each other, during which Elle had to bend over double and Kylie sprang into the air – but Kylie managed it; for the record, she and Elle look equally sensational.

The accompanying interview reveals little – when asked who the most famous Australian woman is, both chant 'Nicole' – but Kylie does let one interesting nugget slip on the subject of men. 'I'd hate to be a guy dating me,' she admits. 'I think, Don't clip my wings. Do not try and pin me down or bind me. I get very protective about my freedom, but at the same time I love the company of a boyfriend. I love being able to share certain things, certain parts of my life with that person. I kind of want the best of both worlds.'

Kylie was also beginning to reassess her brief indie period in a different light. 'I was in danger of becoming a post-ironic pet for alternative artists,' she stated bluntly. 'I think what my public really wants is pure Kylie.' They were about to get it, too. Kylie had not spent that long label-less: Parlophone, which could see a good thing when it gyrated towards them in hot pants, had signed Kylie and work had begun on a new album, an album that would in many ways be back to basics. This had clearly healed some wounds and allowed Kylie to look back on the recent past with more equanimity.

'I parted with deConstruction after a long and mainly happy time together because we didn't achieve what we wanted to achieve with the last album,' she said diplomatically. 'There are no fingers being pointed. I made mistakes, they made mistakes. It was a harmonious split for both parties and at no point did I consider it to be the end of my musical career. Besides, I wasn't without a deal for long. I shopped around for six months before I signed with Parlophone. Musically, I won't be foolish and go back to somewhere I've been, but I am going down that pop route because that is when I am at my best.'

These were brave words. Kylie might not have thought her career was finished, but there were some voices in the industry who were saying just that, and it was going to take time to get herself back to where she once had been. She went back to work with renewed determination: giving interviews, meeting industry figures and charming everyone she encountered. She was still experimenting and taking risks, too: in 1999 she appeared in a production of *The Tempest* in Barbados with the actor Rupert Penry-Jones. 'We were playing the lovers Ferdinand and Miranda,' said Rupert, 'so naturally we got on very well.'

They certainly did. Rupert, like many of Kylie's amours, is tall, very good looking and has worked as a model, and so it was only a matter of time before life started imitating art. The relationship only lasted for a short while but would seem to have made a lasting impression on Rupe: 'She's one of the most incredible people I've met,' he said. 'I thought I was one of the luckiest men in the world and, to be honest, I can't believe it lasted more than a week. She's a very free spirit. I don't think she's ever going to belong to anybody.' The romance was initially secret until the couple were spotted attending a performance of the ancient Greek play *Antigone* – 'I don't think I'll try anything like this on the stage, at least not for a while,' chirped Kylie. 'I'm only here as a punter. It felt like hard work, though, didn't it?'

Rupert found the attention hard to bear and wanted to keep it quiet. 'One part of me wanted to scream it from the rooftops,' he said later. 'But the other side of me thought it better to say nothing.' The couple's relationship was confirmed, though, when Kylie was spotted on the back of Rupert's motorbike as the couple whizzed around Stratford-Upon-Avon; passers-by noticed that Kylie was wearing socks instead of gloves. But again, the relationship didn't last. Kylie the free spirit wanted to break free and Kylie the workaholic had a new project to get on with. She was about to make one of the most sensational comebacks in British pop history – and it was all down to a pair of golden pants.

11

Spinning Around

The release of 'Spinning Around' marked the moment that Kylie re-established herself as the über pop kitten of the day. It came out in the summer of 2000 and finally put Kylie where she wanted to be: back at number one both in the charts and the hearts of the nation. The single's success also made the *Guinness Book of Records*, as it marked the first time an Australian female solo artist had debuted at number one in the UK charts.

Kylie was now an old lady of 32, though, and so the doom mongers were out in force: was she going to be able to compete with youngsters like 19-year-old Britney Spears? 'I think we've got slightly different markets, mine might be a little older,' said Kylie tactfully. 'Obviously we're competing in that radio adds a few songs a week and there's only ten songs in the top ten and everyone wants to be in there, and there's always someone who is on fire at the moment. Currently it's Britney. But,' she added, 'I know a lot of my fanbase are thinking, Great, move over everyone, she's back.'

She certainly was. 'Spinning Around' was pure Kylie: easy-listening pop with an absolutely sensational video to back it up. Kylie knew that a lot was riding on this and went all out for it. During the video, which portrayed people dancing in a nightclub, Kylie sports two outfits: a pair of white hot pants with a red top and a pair of gold hot pants with a gold top. The latter made such a deep impression on the public consciousness that they are remembered – by men, at least – with a positive longing, to say nothing of lustfulness.

Poor Kylie subsequently had to put up with drooling on a major scale, not least from comic Frank Skinner, who offered her £50,000 for the shorts. Given that Kylie had bought them in a market for 50p about five years previously it would have been, as she herself observed, a good investment – though one that she politely declined to cash in.

'Well, it's some people's favourite bit,' said Kylie on the question of her bottom's starring role in her video. 'There is a bit of a story to this. One of my producers, Johnny Douglas, said he really liked the video for "Some Kind Of Bliss" and I asked why and he said, "Well, it was the little denim hot pants." So I made a mental note. The concept for the video is basically people having fun in a nightclub and I just thought: hot pants.'

No one can do sex kitten like Kylie, and nowhere is this more apparent than in that 'Spinning Around' video. She doesn't so much dance as undulate, while her accompanying dancers writhe slowly in the background: close your eyes ever so slightly and you could almost be watching the preliminary scenes of an orgy rather than people having a bop. Men absolutely loved it – and so, according to la Minogue, did women.

'When "Spinning Around" came out, I was so surprised,' she admitted. 'So many girls and women came up to me and said,

"We love your song, you look so great and sexy in that video."
And it really touched me that they weren't saying, "Huh,
what's she doing strutting around in those shorts making all of
us feel insecure?" I was their mate.'

Certainly, over the years, Kylie has established a relationship
with her audience that is more complicated and goes deeper
than the usual bond between star and fan. She is aware of that
herself. 'I imagine to a lot of people I'm like a sister or a distant
relative you know about but have never met,' she says. 'I've got
relatives like that. So you have some connection. They've seen
all my ups and downs and blunders. Growing up in public
could have been disastrous, but somehow it's brought the
audience and me closer together. They relate their experiences
to mine.'

There is a great deal of truth in that, but the fact that Kylie
remains an astonishingly attractive woman doesn't work
against her, either. It was around the time of 'Spinning
Around' that her bottom became a national obsession. The
British have always loved bottoms and confronted with one of
the pertest and prettiest examples on the planet, they could
scarcely contain their joy. One interviewer rather ungallantly
asked Kylie if she had used a stunt bum in the video: 'It's me,'
said Kylie. 'I guess everyone's surprised because I'm supposed
to be an old woman by now.'

And although Kylie sometimes gets a bit tired of the
attention received by her derrière, she often can't resist playing
it up for all she's worth. At around the time of the 'Spinning
Around' video, she was also pictured on the cover of the men's
magazine GQ recreating that famous Athena poster in the
1970s, in which a decorative tennis player, back to the camera,
lifts her skirt to reveal nothing but a perfect posterior
underneath. Kylie complained that the magazine had

airbrushed out her knickers, but no one cared: she looked even better than her greatest fans could have imagined. 'I just saw GQ and my heart went ... even I'm shocked, and I knew what to expect,' she said afterwards.

'It's a three-quarter-page pic of my bum. It's quite odd. I'm getting older, I'd have thought I wouldn't be doing that stuff anymore, but so many times I'll be doing photo shoots and I end up in my knickers. I'm a very natural flirt, but I don't see it in a sexual way – a lot of the time I'm like an over-excited puppy. I think I'm being friendly with someone, they think I'm flirting with them.'

Now that Kylie had rediscovered not only success, but also the kind of work she wanted to be doing, she was able to reflect on the period that had caused her some problems. 'It was difficult, it was frustrating, I definitely had happier times in my life, but in retrospect I am thankful for what it taught me and what it brought out of me at the time,' she mused.

'"Spinning Around" was exactly what I needed at that time and I don't think I appreciated how important that record was then because I had every confidence it would work just because of how easily that album had come around. The people I was working with, the enthusiasm the talent – everything that was thrown into that pot was good. So I thought it would work, just didn't know it would be quite as successful as it was, which was a fantastic surprise. Now I realise if it had not worked I would be in a very different position right now, so "Spinning Around" became a best friend for a while.'

And then there was the follow-up album: *Light Years*, which was a full-on return to her pop past. It was pure Kylie: camp, disco and a lot of fun. The magazine *Rolling Stone* commented that given her immediate past, the attitude behind it came out quite strongly as 'Fuck Art, Let's Dance.'

Kylie agreed. 'I've been much happier doing this album,' she said. 'I actually can't believe it's done. The whole thing felt like a summer holiday, especially compared to the last album, where it was one problem after another. When I first met the different writers and producers for this one I said, "These are my key words: poolside, beach, cocktails and disco." And I think we did it. I wanted to get back to what I do best and I learned that lesson mainly by doing that tour in Australia. I could actually feel for myself and see what the audience responded to, what they wanted. When I signed with Parlophone, we all wanted the same thing. There was a really good momentum, it wasn't too laboured or rushed, I wasn't sitting around thinking: What are they doing? Hello? Yoo-hoo!'

Although she had put her unfortunate experiences to good use, Kylie clearly didn't want to go through such a trying time again in a hurry. 'It's much easier to be working on something that's successful,' she reasoned. 'I couldn't do that slog again. I wanted to work on something that was fun. And just about everyone I worked with, aside from their talent, they're funny! We'd just be tittering and giggling in the studio and some of the lyrics we've gotten away with are really funny.'

Kylie particularly enjoyed recording the track 'Your Disco Needs You': one line goes 'kick your ass', at which the backing singers chime in with 'aaaaassssss.' 'That's a goooooooood backing vocal, isn't it?' said a delighted Kylie. 'They had 10 male vocalists and they tracked them about three times so you've got 30 beefy vocalists going, 'aaaaassssss!' I think they were slightly embarrassed.'

To add to all the fun, Kylie wrote a couple of songs with Robbie Williams, with whom she also duetted. Robbie had been very keen for the two of them to work together – fittingly so, given that the two were emerging as two of pop's greatest survivors. They were also both considered to be heart-throbs – and both had had tangled and complicated love lives in the past. To cap it all, Robbie, like Kylie, had never managed to find a lasting relationship. So how did Robbie behave when they got together in the studio? Was Kylie subjected to the famous Williams charm?

'I think he's quite naughty a lot of the time,' said Kylie coyly. 'He was pretty well behaved with me in the studio. Especially with the song we did for his album, which is gonna be on my album as well, now. Robbie's Robbie. Not only is he a great pop star, but he is a great songwriter. He came up with the title "Your Disco Needs You" and that's how that one happened. Then I said I'd love to have a song called "Loveboat" and we did it. That simple.'

By this time Kylie was dating the model James Gooding, of which more later, but the relationship was not yet widely known about and so there was some speculation about whether Kylie and Robbie were romantically involved. The video for Robbie's single 'Kids' was a riot, and ended up with the two of them naked in a swimming pool. Given that both had active and well-documented love lives, were they getting it on in real life? The answer was, 'In Robbie's dreams.' And he did try – 'Kylie, do you fancy a good sex session?' he asked publicly – but Kylie wasn't interested.

'Well basically, I fancy her,' said Robbie, who also confessed to being extremely nervous when they met. 'I always have and it's a kick for me. She's a fantastic singer with a lot of personality. Great charisma. I was like, "Kylie, I fancy you – can you sing on my record please?" I was really nervous when we got together to sing the duet. I couldn't even speak to her.

I could sing with her but that's Robbie singing – Robbie can sing with anyone. Robbie's brave.'

'Kids' reached number two in the charts. About a year later, Kylie gave an interview in which she said she regretted not dating Robbie. 'Robbie has always said that I am his ideal woman,' she said. 'And I have always felt that he is gorgeous, attractive and totally interesting. I always felt it might have happened, that we might have been a couple. But I think the time has passed now. It just never happened, which I feel is a shame. But what can I do? We have been friends for so long we can't really go backwards in life. Now we are just the best of friends.'

That's one way of looking at it, anyway. Some time later, Kylie gave an interview in which she admitted what had really been going on. 'I had a boyfriend through all of that [the rumpus surrounding her and Robbie] and Robbie wasn't able to cut through that. I haven't actually seen Rob in ages. I think we both know how to play up to the camera and that really was all there was to it. There was certainly a chemistry when we were working but beyond that … he's a good guy who makes me laugh.'

At the end of her best year ever, GQ awarded Kylie the GQ Services To Mankind Award. Thanking the magazine and its readers, Kylie wrote a highly entertaining piece about her year, which included some revealing snapshots about the lives of the rich and famous. 'Sometimes I think that if Robbie stopped actively looking for happiness, it might just come along,' she wrote. 'The work we've done together has been pretty tight scheduled so we've only had a chance to have a couple of heart to hearts – real personal moments – but I know a lot about the business he's in. On that level, I get him and could talk to him about that stuff. But I'm sure that

Robert Peter Williams – as opposed to Rob – is a highly complex individual and I would love to sit and have a proper conversation with him one day. I think I might be able to help him in certain areas.

'My favourite moment with Robbie was when I appeared at his show in Manchester. It was just priceless because Rob's so in control on stage, he's almost impossible to rattle. But he hadn't seen the dress I was going to wear – it was the little silver slip of a thing that I wore at the MTV Awards too – but his face was absolutely beautiful because for a second he completely lost it. All the super-confidence was suddenly stripped away and he was like, "Unnghh!" It was excellent. As soon as I was out of sight he was back in control but just for a minute there he was sweating. I loved it.'

Kylie also had an encounter with Prince Charles. 'A friend recently asked what he smelled like, but how should I know? I didn't sniff him. I was sitting next to him at a *Vogue* dinner and I'm sure he was wearing some very expensive and exclusive cologne, but I'm not a sniffer dog. Although having said that, I made just about every other faux pas possible. I didn't know what to call him – I mean, I knew not to call him Chas – but I think in the most formal sense you're supposed to refer to him as Your Royal Highness in as much as you can't call him "you". So I was supposed to say, "And what does your Royal Highness think of the soup?" But I just couldn't do that. I tried but it was too much to remember. All that etiquette.

'He had Camilla with him but she sat at the next table, which is kind of nice, but there's a total method to the way everything is done with the royals. Although I was beside him it was made pretty obvious that I was due to be spoken to during the second half of the meal. So for the first half he spoke to the editor of *Vogue*, then he subtly turned round and started talking to me. But it's all very smoothly done and he's a very skilled conversationalist. He made me feel at ease and he listened as I was gabbling on and on. I wonder if he has any recollection of the evening?' (Kylie was being disingenuous here, surely.) 'I came away with the impression that he is very, very good at his job.

'My one regret about meeting him is that I said the word "penis",' she revealed. 'We were talking about Sir Les Patterson and I said, "Oh I did a show with Sir Les and we sang 'Where The Wild Roses Grow' but he got his penis out in the middle of the song and started chasing me around the stage." I was telling Charles this whole story and he was really laughing. He found it genuinely funny. It was only the next day I woke up and thought, Oh my God, I said "penis" to a prince!'

All told, 2000 had been a very, very good year, but the best was yet to come. The twenty-seventh Olympic Games, to be staged in Sydney in September, effectively turned out to be Kylie's coronation as the Princess of Pop. And she revelled in it. It was a monumentally star-studded occasion, with a pre-split Tom Cruise and Nicole Kidman in attendance, alongside Leonardo diCaprio, Calista Flockhart, Arnold Schwarzenegger, Peter Gabriel, Kate Bush, Paul Hogan, Elle Macpherson, Chelsea Clinton, Bill Gates, Rupert Murdoch, others too numerous to mention – and Kylie Minogue.

Kylie was the star of the show. She performed at the para-lympics and the opening and closing ceremony of the main attraction to 180,000 in the stadium, her biggest live audience ever, and four billion worldwide. Kylie's entrance was as spectacular as everything else about the day: she was borne on to the stage on a giant surfboard held aloft by footballers.

Dressed in the manner of a Las Vegas showgirl, with a bright pink outfit topped by a pink feather head-dress, she performed 'Spinning Around', 'Celebration', 'On A Night Like This' and 'Dancing Queen', all of which received rapturous applause from the audience. 'The most incredible moment had to be performing at the closing ceremony of the Olympics in Sydney,' she wrote in her GQ piece. 'I was so desperate to be involved in the games because I was just so proud that they were being held in my country.

'Technically it could have been a nightmare. I was carried on to the stage on a surfboard which was held aloft by Australian footballers – not dancers, who know how to do that sort of thing, but Australian footballers – so I was very nervous. But once I was on stage it was unbelievable. It's actually very hard for me to convey in words what it was like. I felt like I was in the middle of some weird special effect when you're dragged out of the dimension you're in. It was just so intense. And funny. There were drag queens everywhere, pawns on bicycles, Elle Macpherson walking out on this massive camera lens … it was just perfect. The whole stadium was just dazzling. For a girl who loves anything that sparkles it was just magical.'

And Kylie finished off with a look back at her new-found happiness. 'The one lesson this year has taught me is that it's OK to be many things,' she wrote. 'I got lost for a while back there. I couldn't be everything I wanted to be so I was just being one side of myself. Now I'm happy with whoever I am on any given day. Come on, I'm a Gemini – you're always dealing with at least two people! So if I've learned something of value – it's how to be myself.'

Rather touchingly, Kylie made a new friend at the Olympics: Nikki Webster, who was just 13 when she too performed to the vast crowd. Nikki, who lives in Sydney, is now playing Dorothy in *The Wizard of Oz*: she and Kylie have kept in touch.

'It all started when we were to climb the Sydney Harbour Bridge together at the time of the Olympics,' recalled Nikki. 'We both got really upset when it was cancelled because of rain. So a group of us went out to dinner. We then did the climb, which we both really loved, and from there we have just kept in contact, which is great. It was so amazing to meet her. She has been one of my idols ever since I was little so for her to be so nice and down to earth was great. "Locomotion" was one of the first songs I ever sang.

'When we first met she asked me a lot about what I wanted to do in my career. She kept e-mailing me and asking me how I was getting along.

'We chat about all different things. When I was doing my new album she asked how it was going. Sometimes Kylie and James e-mail me together. Kylie and I have funny little names for each other – little code names. My e-mail name is "tiny star" and she will write "to my little chick". Kylie is just such a beautiful person and really helpful. She told me if I ever needed any help she was on the other end of the phone and would always be there.

'It was great to have someone who is so successful looking out for me when I was starting my career. I was speaking to her parents at a charity ball and they said that Kylie was interested in me because I am so young and she is trying to look after my rights. Kylie and James are going very well. She hasn't asked me to be a bridesmaid – but it would be fun.' sadley, it was not to be. Kylie and James were to break up in highly acrimonious circumstances.

12

We Are Family

I spend all day every day
working towards being famous
DANNII MINOGUE

If there has been one constant about Kylie's Minogue's
life, it is the endless speculation about her relationship
with her younger sister Dannii. It was Dannii, of course, who
first made it to the big time in Australia, but in the
intervening years, she has been well and truly eclipsed by her
older sister Kylie. And yet the parallels in their lives are there
for all to see: both started on Australian soaps, both then went
on to forge musical careers for themselves and both have had
turbulent love lives. They both now live in London; Dannii
was for a time managed by Terry Blamey, who is Kylie's
manager; they both have their own clothing range; and they
are both extremely ambitious.

To cap it all, the physical resemblance is strong: both are
petite with good bone structure and wide mouths. The main
difference these days is hair colour – Dannii's brunette to
Kylie's blonde – although some uncharitable commentators
have remarked that Dannii's resemblance to Kylie is a good
deal stronger than it was 10 years ago, when Dannii weighed
a lot more than she does now. There were also rumours,

always fiercely denied, that in 1996 Dannii had breast implants, boosting her figure from 34B to 36D.

'I think people are fascinated talking about it,' snapped Dannii to an interviewer when the subject came up some years later. 'The thing I do find weird is being asked about it. If the situation were reversed I wouldn't be asking you anything about your penis or what you do with it. When you're doing a lot of photo sessions you see lots of images of yourself and get bored of the way you look – that's why I change my hair colour a lot. Although I once dyed my hair red just for a birthday party, I was told it would wash straight out – of course it didn't and I was a permanently red colour, which I absolutely hated.'

The real difference between the two sisters is temperament. Dannii is wild, upfront and confrontational; Kylie is polite, reserved and, when she can, avoids fights. The pair say they are good friends and yet the doubts linger on: can there really be no rivalry between them? Wasn't it galling for Kylie to see her little sister achieve stardom before she did? And didn't Dannii resent being so comprehensively overtaken by her big sis? The answer to both of those questions would certainly be yes in the vast majority of families – and yet the sisters firmly deny that anything is or ever has been amiss between the two of them. All, according to the two girls, is sisterly bliss.

Of course, as Kylie herself has never forgotten, Dannielle Jane Minogue was originally the star in the family and she also beat Kylie in the race to the altar, although her marriage didn't last. She joined *The Sullivans* aged seven – after Kylie had had a role in the programme – went on to present *Young Talent Time* and ended up in the soap *Home and Away* as Emma, all before turning up in London in 1991 to promote

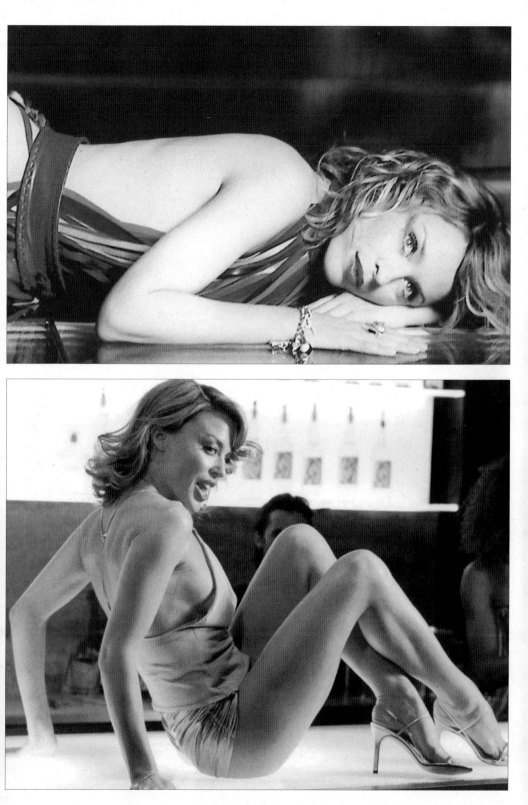

Kylie is well known for her risqué outfits, the gold hot pants shown here have even inspired art. In 2003 an artist displayed a lifesize picture of her in these hot pants in the window of his gallery. The picture proved quite a distraction to passers by!

Kylie with James Gooding, the gorgeous couple eventually parted after several years together.

Kylie performed with Justin Timberlake at the Brit Awards in 2003. Rumours later circulated about their after-show antics.

Kylie with her new beau, the French actor, Olivier Martinez.

In 2003, Kylie launched her own exciting range of lingerie. She is pictured here at the 'Love Kylie' launch.

Above: Her waxwork is one of the most popular at London's Madame Tussauds. The skimpy outfit pictured here was eventually replaced with a longer dress due to complaints about its suitability for a family attraction.

Below: The museum faced further criticism in 2004 when they staged a celebrity nativity scene featuring Kylie as the Angel.

Back in business! A radiant Kylie makes a return to public life in the summer of 2006.

Top: Kylie did signing sessions for the release of her book *The Showgirl Princess*.

Bottom: Kylie and Jake Shears from the Scissor Sisters after a show by the band in September 2006.

her single 'Love and Kisses'. She loved *Young Talent Time*. 'There was a talent school attached to it,' she recalls. 'Lots of kids went with their pushy mothers, hoping to get them on stage. I just went because I loved the classes, the singing and dancing, and that's what got me the job in the end.' Demonstrating the determination that the Minogue girls have shown throughout their lives, she worked on it six days a week. 'When I did that show it was Kylie who was trying to live down being in my shadow,' Dannii once remarked. 'In Australia, people know who I am and I am secure in my identity. We're sisters, we love each other, we get along great, so it is natural I should be happy for her.'

And though Dannii has not matched Kylie in terms of success since then, she's certainly been busy: she appeared in the film *Secrets*, she's been a TV presenter for the Disney Channel and *The Big Breakfast*, she's designed her own range of bikinis, appeared in the biggest selling calendar of 1997, taken the parts of Rizzo in the musical *Grease*, Lady Macbeth in the Scottish play and Esmerelda in *Notre Dame de Paris* and between all this managed to fit in a 17-month-long marriage to fellow *Home and Away* star Julian McMahon, son of the former Australian prime minister Sir William McMahon, with whom she tied the knot when she was just 22. Confused? We've hardly started. Dannii has been fiercely ambitious practically from the moment she crawled from the cradle: 'I was seven when I heard a record for the first time and I thought Wow, that's what I want to do,' she once revealed.

She also has her own website, www.dannii.com, 'the website for all your Dannii needs, which Dannii herself helps to write.' Be sure, however, to remember the second 'i' if you want to visit it – 'Because there's a famous porn site called www.danni.com, and you don't want to go spelling it wrong,' explains the youngest Minogue. 'Apparently she gets more hits than any other porn site and it may just be people looking for me.'

All told it's not surprising that Dannii gets irritated by the constant comparisons with her big sister: 'I don't like being pigeonholed into one thing,' she says. 'I like doing a mixture of things and not getting bored. I've done all these things for 20 years. I'd never like to be asked to choose just one to call my career. I'm a workaholic and a control freak.' That's not all she is, according to the writer John Walsh:

'Ever since she was seven, she's been performing like billyo,' he wrote, 'unceasingly, unstoppably – acting, singing, dancing, writing, going blonde, going brunette, slimming down, fronting up, being measured against her big sister Kylie, transforming herself in to a lads' mag cover girl sex pot along the lines of the world's most downloaded woman, even getting her kit off for Australian *Playboy* – until, ironically, she is now known more for being an unclassifiable, polymorphous celeb than for anything more specific.'

The real problem, according to friends of the family, stems back to that very early audition for *The Sullivans* – the audition that was meant only for Dannii, until Kylie tagged along too. Kylie is open about what happened, as related in Chapter One. 'Danielle had been spotted in a shop by someone who arranged for her to try out for *The Sullivans*,' she said in an interview given just after she became famous. 'Mum said I'd have to go along, too or none of us were going. We all went off to the studio and I got the part intended for Danielle.'

It was all rather unfortunate – for Dannii, at least. Dannii, of course, joined the show later and for some time overtook her older sister in the fame stakes. But when Kylie found success with *Neighbours*, old wounds were reopened and

Dannii made her feelings quite plain. 'Danielle has never forgiven Kylie for stealing the part which would have brought her real acting stardom,' said a family friend a couple of years after Kylie hit the big time. 'Instead she was left in limbo year after year as a variety starlet.' Kylie herself added at the time, 'I'd rather not talk about my relationship with Danielle.' Dannii didn't help matters when she announced she never watched *Neighbours* – 'I just don't have the time.'

By 1990, the sisters had sorted things out considerably, with Dannii reflecting on their relationship then and now. 'Kylie and I fought a lot when we were younger,' she admitted. 'We shared a room and divided it with a piece of string directly down the middle. All her things were on one side and all mine on the other. She couldn't come on to my side and I couldn't go on to hers or there would be a lot of trouble. In many ways it was very difficult sharing a room with her and we often got on each other's nerves.

'But I also looked up to her a lot. I desperately wanted to be involved with her friends because they were so hip and groovy. Yet she'd say, "No, you can't muck around with us, go away!" Her music is bubble gum pop – you can't read any more in to it. It's not what I'd want to do, though. Kids love her music and it's fun, but I wouldn't want to put it on and play it all the time.' But over time the sisters had become close, Dannii revealed. 'Kylie's always there for me if I want to pour my heart out.'

And as for that other potential area of rivalry, there was no problem. 'Kylie and I have never been rivals over boyfriends, thank goodness,' Dannii says. 'We've never been around the same boys except Jason Donovan. I've known him since I was 15 but have never fancied him. He's just a close friend of mine.'

It didn't help that the two have been involved in so many similar projects. Even if the girls didn't want to compare themselves to each other, they were given no choice by the rest of the industry, which did. Just as Kylie became known to the British public through one Australian soap opera, her little sister did exactly the same with another: *Home and Away*. The soap's bosses drew the parallel just in case anyone was in any doubt as to Dannii's role on the show: 'It's make-or-break time,' said a cheery insider on the show following the news that Dannii had been signed up. 'We're banking on Dannii to wow you Poms, just like Kylie did in *Neighbours*.' It is a mark of how complex the sisters' relationship is, incidentally, that there are rumours that Dannii almost turned down the part of the wild punkette Emma for fear of upsetting her sister. Kylie, according to the gossip at the time, was unbothered. 'The world is big enough for two Minogues,' was all Dannii would say.

As it happened, this was the year Kylie was starring in *The Delinquents* – not her finest hour and not really a time at which she would relish comparisons being made. There was, however, no avoiding them. The powers that be behind *Home and Away* were milking the Minogue name for all it was worth, and were only too happy to come up with other points of reference in case anyone else might have missed them. 'Kylie Minogue's little sister Dannii is all set to show the Aussie superstar a fling or two with her first steamy sex romps – described as some of the hottest scenes shown on TV,' drooled one writer.

'Dannii, 18, will set screens alight in the no-holds-barred soap *Home and Away* where she plays a love-hungry man-stealer. Her frank beach love-making with heart-throb teen star Matt Stevenson as Adam will make Kylie's exploits in her raunchy film *Delinquents* [sic] look like "kids' stuff" according to producers of the hit soap.'

And so it went on, with Matt dragged in to talk about the plot and the producers yet again highlighting the relationship between the girls when they added, 'Dannii is very adult in her approach to acting and really sizzles in the beach scenes with Matt.' It would have caused a strain between the closest of siblings and given that Kylie and Dannii had been competing for the same parts pretty much since crawling out of the cradle, one can only imagine the effect it would have had on the two.

And there were all sorts of other crossovers. Dannii's first boyfriend was Paul Goldman, a video director who used to work with Jason Donovan. For some time they shared a manager, Terry Blamey. Like Kylie, Dannii's made movies and records and then there was that appearance in Grease – the musical that so inspired her sister. Everywhere Dannii went – with the exception of matrimony and musicals – Kylie had been before. Who could blame them for feeling a little tense?

The sisters, however, were clearly beginning to realise that the repeated talk of rivalry was damaging to both of them – after all, it's very uncool to be portrayed as being jealous of anyone, especially your own flesh and blood – and were finally trying to mount some form of damage control. It might also have occurred to Dannii that the constant comparisons to Kylie could well backfire on her – as indeed they probably have done in the longer term – and so a new image of the two – fond of each other and yet entirely independent – began to emerge.

Dannii was also beginning to discover what it was like to live in Kylie's shadow rather than the other way round. 'I've never been jealous of Kylie's success,' she said firmly, when

Kylie was in her first flush of fame. 'I think what has happened to her is great – it couldn't have been planned better. She's only 21 but she's done so much. Everything's been perfect for her. No, I don't envy her, although I must admit I'd like to do something like her latest film – that looks really fun.'

Dannii also began to face accusations that she was only getting attention because she was a Minogue. 'I could have done what I'm doing without Kylie,' she stated for the record. 'And I don't want to go the same way she's going. She's never sat down with me and said, "Dannii you should do this", or, "You shouldn't do that." If I asked her she'd give me advice, in the same way that I'd give her advice if she asked me for any. But Kylie has given me a few tips on acting. A lot of people may try to use me but I talked all this over with my parents and we picked a good manager who looks after Kylie, too.'

Dannii certainly realised that her role in *Home and Away* represented a good opportunity for her and, famous sister or no, that it would have been madness to mess it up. That Minogue professionalism went into full swing and Dannii leapt in to her new role with gusto. '*Home and Away* was originally supposed to be just a 13-week run, which turned into a year,' she revealed after leaving the soap. 'The show was gruelling, producing two and a half hours of TV a week. I went in the dark and came back in the dark, up at 4 a.m. and back at 9 p.m., then I'd have to learn the next day's lines.' And make no mistake – she came through like a pro.

That mutual manager also led to suggestions, often repeated throughout the sisters' careers, that they should record something together. Neither Minogue appeared to be keen. 'Kylie and I used to sing together at home when we were little but we've no plans to make a single at the moment,' said

Dannii at one point. 'I'm just interested in establishing my own career. But I'm not new to this business. Even when I was acting at seven, because I couldn't get stage gear to fit me, I used to design my own and my grandmother would make them up! If I hadn't chosen an acting and singing career, I think I would have gone in to the fashion industry full time.'

'It gets really boring when people keep implying that Kylie and I dislike each other,' said Dannii wearily on one occasion. 'We're going to write some songs together this year and it will be a big "up yours" to everyone who thinks we're bitter rivals.'

But still a slight tension pervades the atmosphere. Dannii is a wilder personality than Kylie, something that has been apparent from a very early age. Not for her the shy and virginal image her sister projected in *Neighbours*: when asked if she could look after herself at school, Dannii replied, 'It helped that I was going out with the school tough guy, which meant I wasn't completely roped in with the nerds. Kylie and my older brother Brendan were at the same school, too, so they'd back me up.'

There were some problems, though. 'I was doing a TV show at the same time I was at school, so I was lumped in with all the nerdy kids with big thick glasses at lunchtime doing my homework – then I could go to rehearsals after school,' she says. 'I was an A+ student in class but I was really naughty. When the work is easy for you it's easier to muck around and not get told off. It's exactly how my personality is now: I like to work hard but I also like to go wild, play jokes on people and be the idiot.'

That wild streak – and perhaps the competitive edge with her sister – came out again when Dannii posed for Australian *Playboy* in 1995, an action some people felt to be ill considered. Dannii was unrepentant. 'I saw it as a compliment they asked me, it was a real ego boost,' she says. 'My dad freaked out but when he saw how beautiful the shots were he came round to the idea. I even had my nan saying she thought they were great.'

The wild image spilled over into her stage performances, not least when it emerged that men had hurled their underwear at her when she was performing live on stage. 'There was one gig where a guy threw a pair of Calvins on to the stage – a magazine reported it and I thought it was funny so for the next few gigs blokes did it again,' relates Dannii, adding, 'I didn't want it to turn in to a whole Tom Jones thing. Big boxers are far less attractive landing on stage than bras and kickers.'

And woe betide the man who annoys Dannii Minogue when she is on stage. 'There were two guys sitting in the front row who were completely out of their heads and just talked the whole way through,' she relates of one performance. 'I could see people in the audience pointing at them and telling them to shut up. But you shouldn't ever fuck with someone with a microphone. For the next song, "So In Love With Yourself", I went down to the front of the stage, stared directly at them and sang the whole song to them. Later in the show they both left and then arrived back together, so I turned to them and said, "I thought it was only girls who went to the toilet together." They just died.'

Like Kylie, Dannii has suffered career lows, something that was rather cruelly pointed out when an interviewer asked her whether appearing in an advertisement for Penguin biscuits was the worst job she'd ever had to do. Dannii rallied bravely. 'Some days on *Home and Away* were pretty grim,' she countered. 'I watch it now from London in the middle of winter and see these beautiful beaches and think maybe it wasn't that bad. But a lot of the time you were handed the script five minutes before you had to record it and told you only had one take. I'd think, What the hell am I doing here?'

Given that the two sisters work in the same field, there is an almost inevitable crossover in what they do. Nowhere was this more apparent than when Dannii took the role of Rizzo in an Australian production of the musical *Grease* opposite Craig McLachlan. Craig, of course, is another ex-*Neighbours* star, while Kylie grew up not only adoring *Grease* but wishing to take on the Olivia Newton-John bad girl persona, something she attempted with a marked lack of success in *The Delinquents*.

Dannii plays down the connection. 'I hate musicals as they're just so old and naff and disgusting,' she says. 'But I grew up when *Grease* the movie came out so John Travolta and Olivia Newton-John were my heroes. It was my first experience of musicals and so I did 70 shows playing to 10,000 people every night. There was a lot of dancing and my legs ended up covered in bruises. When I went to get my legs waxed the woman must have thought my boyfriend was beating me up.' Kylie was generous about her sister's performance. 'She was a good Rizzo too!' she said. 'And that very concisely sums up the differences between us – she always wanted to be Rizzo, I always wanted to be Sandy!'

And where Dannii has something else in common with Kylie is that neither seems to have been able to settle down in her personal life. Dannii's marriage to Julian ended years ago and like her older sister, she's had a stream of boyfriends, including, more or less in this order, Paul Goldman, who used to direct Jason Donovan's videos, a singer called Whycliffe, a model called Sean, her husband Julian, Mark Ellis, a City banker, photographer Steve Shaw, Formula One World

Championship winner Jacques Villeneuve – to whom she was briefly engaged – Michael Edwards-Hammond, of whom more below and, as at the time of writing, Craig Logan, the former Bros bassist, to whom she is engaged.

'When it comes to men, Kylie and I are just opposites in every way,' reveals Dannii. 'She likes scruffy-looking and natural men, the ones who are always on the move, the dreamers. I like clean-cut men who know where they are going. I like them to be in control of their lives. I also like the idea of committing for life but Kylie is more spontaneous with her choice of boyfriends. She is more here, there and everywhere and can get bored with a man in a second. I like to really get stuck in to a relationship.

'But many men have shied away from my controlling nature. I'm not perfect. I have always lived by my own rules and tried to learn from my mistakes. Our parents taught Kylie and me that. But like a lot of Australian women, I don't take any nonsense from men. We are as tough as nails and independent. I am opinionated and it's never hard for me to tell a man he's wrong. I like to run the show and that scares men, sometimes.'

In 1999, in an attempt to squash the rivalry rumours, once and for all, the two sisters gave an interview to *Esquire* magazine. Would they, asked the interviewer – getting straight to the nitty gritty – ever steal each other's boyfriends? 'No,' said Dannii firmly. 'We go for such different guys. Don't even fancy the same ones.' And what is Kylie's type? 'Kylie likes a challenge,' said Dannii. 'Someone who isn't going to kiss her feet. Am I wrong? No, see. She wants someone who is going to really stimulate her, intellectually or artistically or whatever. And she does like a bit of a rogue.'

'Absolutely right, Dan,' agreed Kylie. 'Let me see. I have

never really thought of her type before. Tall is the first thing that springs to mind. She once had a boyfriend who was six feet four or five and thank God, that relationship didn't last long because family photos would have been a nightmare – we are all short. So he would have had to spend his life on his knees. So, tall – stable. I am thinking of Steve [Dannii's then boyfriend, photographer Stephen Shaw] here. Funny. Humorous, I should say. Artistic.'

Then came the big question: which one is the bigger flirt? Kylie's hand shot up. 'Always has been,' said Dannii. 'Anyone and anything. Male or female. She'll flirt with it.' 'It's just part of what I am,' said Kylie coyly. 'It does get me into trouble.' 'But it's not a sexual thing,' Dannii butted in hastily. 'More a mischievous, naughty approach.' 'I do get excited and childish – still – before I go into a club or bar,' interjected Kylie who, as it happens, was sounding more excited and childish as the interview wore on. 'At one point I tried to bottle it up and suppress it, but it didn't work. I couldn't be someone I wasn't.'

And so now on to temperament. Which has the shorter fuse? 'I do,' says Dannii rather surprisingly. 'But I think we are both capable of putting people in their place. Most of the time the public are so nice but once in a while they, especially the guys, can be so rude and obnoxious and they just don't expect a small, pretty girl to come right back at them. I think British girls won't stand up for themselves, whereas we're Aussie girls. I will not let someone treat me the way I don't want to be treated.'

Kylie adds, 'I think Dan can be stronger, more forceful. I think I have quieter strength. But yes, there are times when I would like to be a little more like her.' 'Whenever people ask me what my sister is like,' said Dannii, 'I think of us as cartoon characters, Kylie is a fluffy, purring pussycat and I'm like a bulldog. Both have their strengths. Sometimes I wish I didn't bulldoze quite as much in every situation. I wish I could be a little more flirty and free. A little more pussycat.'

For what it is worth, Dannii is the more physically adventurous – 'It comes from being the youngest and following my brother, trying to keep up with him and his mates. Boys will ride a bike down a hill without any thought of the fact they will crash at the bottom. I started to be the same' – and the one who's keen on cars, while Kylie is more of a taxi girl herself. It then emerged that the girls can think of only one row between them in their lives: when Kylie came home and caught Dannii wearing her clothes.

'Well,' explained Kylie, 'when you are 14 or 15 you are very possessive about clothes, especially if your little sister has them on. It was, "That's mine", but you grow out of it. Now we're Jackie and Joan, darling.' (It would seem that Kylie was not trying to impart a veiled message here – she just didn't know that the Collins sisters are rumoured to be as big a rival of each other as ... well, the Minogue sisters.) And then, having received the news that they are taller than expected – 'We love you,' trilled Kylie – the two rushed off into the rain.

Certainly, the Minogue sisters do a great deal to support one another in public. Dannii turned up for the televised *An Audience With Kylie Minogue* in 2001 and shouted and applauded with the best of them. Kylie, meanwhile, showed up on the opening night of *Notre Dame de Paris*, based on the Victor Hugo novel, in which Dannii was starring as Esmeralda. 'I can't wait to see the show. I am so excited for her,' said Kylie. 'I think this is something she really excels at. I am just really glad to be here tonight with my brother

Brendan and my parents will be over here in a few weeks, so it will be a real family affair.'

The role was a success for Dannii, but with a bitter-sweet edge. Dannii had briefly found romance with theatre producer Michael Edwards-Hammond, but the relationship ended at his instigation and a dreadfully upset Dannii was off sick for two weeks, after which she decided not to renew her contract when it came up after six months.

Since then, Kylie has been increasingly generous towards her little sister – perhaps, given her new-found status as icon, she can afford to be. In 2002 she said of Dannii, 'I used to be very competitive with her when I was younger. People ask who I think is the sexiest and I have to say her. And she is taller than me.'

Equally, Kylie's success in later years has reflected well on her little sister. Since watching Kylie turn herself from mid-Nineties embarrassment to early Noughties überbabe, Dannii has also begun to reshape her singing career. After she sang on Riva's hit single 'Who Do You Love Now?', which reached number two, London Records outbid five other labels to sign Dannii up for a six-album deal. The deal, said a spokesperson, was worth a 'huge amount'.

But still the fascination about the sisters' relationship persist. An assistant in one of Kylie's favourite shops, VV Rouleaux atelier in Sloane Street, which sells ribbons, trimmings and braids (and which is also a favourite with Dannii), observes: 'They never come in to the shop together – always separately. They are quite similar although Dannii is more friendly than Kylie and looks a lot older.'

Kylie probably came closest to the truth of what lies behind a clearly complex relationship when asked what would happen if Dannii got to number one and she didn't. What would she do? 'I'll cross that bridge when and where,' said Kylie. 'I'll screen my calls! Ha, ha. No, she knows I'm there if she needs me. I think we both have feelings for one another bordering on jealousy and admiration.'

Clearly, the pattern has repeated itself throughout their lives: when they were children, Kylie muscled in on Dannii's act and got the part she wanted and as an adult, she just can't help stealing the limelight. Kylie has over-shadowed Dannii; it's a fact. But then again, Kylie has overshadowed just about everyone: Jason Donovan, Victoria Beckham, with whom she battled in the charts, Gisele Bundchen – the two posed for a photograph and Kylie came out best – and if he'd lived, she'd more than likely have ended up overshadowing Michael Hutchence, too. As for Dannii, she's talented, good looking and has done a lot with her life already. And who could ask for more than that?

13

Is Kylie An Alien?

I could see myself as a glitter hippy
KYLIE MINOGUE

Kylie Minogue has always been aware of her looks. Closely resembling her mother, Kylie is tiny – 5'1" – and that hairstyle from her *Neighbours* days, which was always assumed to be a perm, is actually her natural hair. It's hardly surprising that she's been constantly conscious of her appearance, though, given that her first appearance on television was at the age of 11 and she was still in her teens when she first began talking about her looks. 'I've proved to myself that I can make an impact,' she said at the age of 18 after she'd become famous in *Neighbours*, 'but I hate being short.' Not that it didn't have some uses. 'Short people,' she observed on another occasion, 'are often very strong minded.'

And of her naturally curly hair? 'A friend and I used to try and straighten our hair with an iron,' she revealed, shortly after that distinctive head of hair had become famous. 'I'd be scared to do anything now, knowing it's such a trademark. I also hate my teeth,' she continued. 'And I don't like my voice but I don't want to have lessons to speak prop-er-lay. It wouldn't be me.' Even Kylie, though, couldn't think of a way of complaining about her weight. 'You wouldn't think I could lose weight,' she once said, 'but I do. I just burn it up.'

It was the *News of the World* that, to Kylie's great amusement, first asked if she was an alien. This was some years ago, before she turned into one of the world's most beautiful Australians, but her looks truly are extraordinary. She is so tiny that she can still sometimes resemble a child: in the video for 'Can't Get You Out Of My Head', for instance, Kylie comes across as part sex siren, part 13-year-old – and even when she waggles that famous bottom, there is as much of the schoolgirl about her as there is of the sex bomb.

Exasperatingly, Kylie doesn't even diet. 'I eat anything I want,' she says. 'My weakness is chocolate, dark chocolate. I seriously don't think it's bad for you.' She was once asked if she ever did Geri Halliwell-style diets: 'I'm so petite it's something I've never done. I mean, if I had any weight fluctuations, no one would know. My work keeps me busy. I can only say what works for me. If you have some chocolate, enjoy it. I mean, what do people in your office think about Geri?' she asked the interviewer. 'There's such an air of determination that goes with her look, you wonder: aren't there any other things she wants to do? It's just so hard to find balance in your life.'

'The thing about Kylie is that she never works out – ever,' says Paul Flynn, editor of *Attitude* magazine. 'She does watch what she eats – she's particularly partial to duck breast – but her only exercise is walking up and down the Kings Road.'

Of course, she does very physical work in her videos and performances, all of which will help keep her slim. Rafael Bonachela, a dancer with the Rambert Dance Company, worked with Kylie for her Brits routine in 2002 and will be choreographing her in the future. 'I was asked to work with

Kylie at the end of 2001 after her creative director, William Baker, saw my last piece for Rambert – Linear Remains, at Sadlers Wells,' Rafael says. 'Kylie is very serious about what she does and works very hard. She is lovely to work with and is open to trying new things. She is incredibly professional and committed and pays great attention to detail.

'I don't know what sort of training she has had before but she is a natural mover, with a great sense of rhythm, and has great flair and picks up new movements quickly and easily. Our time together is very focused on rehearsing so we talk about the movements, the style and the feel of whatever performance she is preparing for. We don't discuss her private life. She has a great sense of humour and is a very sweet person.'

Will Baker is not just Kylie's creative director. He also is her stylist, an association that goes back to 1994 when he was working in Vivienne Westwood's shop at the age of 19. He had wanted to be Kylie's stylist ever since he saw her in 'What Do I Have To Do', so when she unexpectedly appeared in the shop one day, Will made the most of his moment. He leapt at his idol, gabbled out ideas, persuaded her to have coffee with him and won the day. The two have worked closely together ever since, becoming close friends in the process. Will does much more than just choose Kylie's outfits: he has an enormous amount of input into which songs are released, with whom she chooses to dance and even the costumes her male dancers wear. The two go shopping together, to haunts such as Portobello Road and Knightsbridge.

Kylie has 'a brilliant sense of style' says Will. 'It's quite eclectic in a way, just very sexy, glamorous. She just kind of picks something up and slings it on and it looks really chic.' 'She's a living Barbie doll,' says shoe designer Patrick Cox. 'All

gay men want to play with her, dress her up, comb her hair.'
BarbieKylie herself is quite aware of this appeal: 'I'm a drag
queen trapped in a woman's body,' she once said. 'A very
short drag queen trapped in a woman's body.'

Uniquely Pete Waterman, Kylie's original mentor and
producer is unmoved by her appeal. 'I'm the only man in the
world who doesn't find her sexy,' he said. 'She's like a
daughter to me. I can't see her in that way and I chuckle when
I see her doing her thing.'

Pete's right: he is alone in not finding Kylie sexy. The man
responsible for much of that sexiness remains Will. He has
coaxed Kylie through innumerable image changes, from
IndieKylie to ComebackKylie to SexKylie and back again.
'Anything we do is a complete collaboration,' he explains. 'It's
not like I tell her how to be; it's a very relaxed process. She's
got all of these different personalities in her head, she's a real
performer and we just work through those. One day she
wants to be a cabaret performer or a glitter queen and it's not
contrived in any way, it's just different sides to her personality.
She's very sexy and quite kitsch, showy but not tacky.
Basically, she's really glamorous. She was born in the wrong
era, she should have been a Hollywood starlet.'

As for the numerous looks Kylie adopts for her videos, Will
says: 'The person Kylie is a product of all her videos she is all
those little characters that she plays. She is everything, she is
all the images that have ever been portrayed and displayed of
her. She is all of those things.' She can even be eccentric, as
Will explained when talking about her video for 'GBI' with
Towa TEI in 1998: 'Kylie is a typeface. I mean she is going: "I
am a typeface" [in the song and video]. It is like it's a
madness. It is a totally deranged video and a totally deranged
idea and she has a totally deranged side. Kylie has a real

insanity, a real –' and here's that word again '– alien-ness about her personality. Sometimes she is very kooky, very eccentric and that comes across in that video more than anything else.'

It was Will who persuaded Kylie to wear the gold hot pants in the 'Spinning Around' video. 'Kylie's bottom is like a peach,' he gushes. 'Sex sells and her best asset is her bum, so let's exaggerate it.' Make-up artist Caroline Barnes supports Will's view. 'She doesn't use anti-cellulite cream – she doesn't need to,' she says. 'It's totally sickening but she doesn't have a scrap of orange peel in sight.' Kylie says she's mystified by all the attention her bottom receives, particularly when clad in those gold hot pants. 'I didn't expect that two years later they would still be getting such attention,' she says. 'It got to the point where I figured the hot pants should go out and do all my interviews for me. I love what Willie's done for me,' she adds. 'I think I should embrace the peach analogy he uses for my bum. It could become a pear rapidly.'

The origins of the miracle that is Kylie's bottom lie in her early childhood. 'It can look all right when it has to,' Kylie admitted once. 'It's funny, it's taken on a life of its own. My brother and sister and I used to have this competition among tickle fights and we'd turn around and go [massive wiggling of backside ensues] – just shake, like that. I always had the movement, the wobbling around. Mine's got the bounce! All those years in the ugly green unitard paid off.'

Will was also responsible for the ensemble Kylie wore to the Brits award, which garnered nearly as much attention as the gold hot pants: a £900 custom-made Dolce & Gabbana mini-dress – not everything Kylie wears is second hand – an £80 pair of Agent Provocateur knickers and some £900 Jimmy Choo boots. 'It's an image,' says Kylie. 'Not reality. Nobody could be like that. When I get home, the stilettos come off, the slippers come on and I become a complete nana.' Julian Macdonald, one of Kylie's favourite designers, also testifies to her ability to step in to the persona of a star. 'When Kylie puts her shoes on,' he says, 'she clicks her heels three times, like Dorothy in *The Wizard Of Oz* – and then she's got that special magic.'

For the record, Kylie has not had a bottom lift, a bottom transplant or any surgery at all on her bum. People who worked with her right at the beginning of her career saw her pertest asset at first hand and can testify to the fact that it hasn't changed to this day. 'I worked with Kylie in 1989 when she first changed her image on the videos "What Do I have To Do" and "Shocked",' says stylist David Thomas. 'It got quite a lot of press coverage and it was when she was going out with Michael Hutchence. I think she was just becoming aware of different things including fashion. When I got the phone call asking me if I would like to work with Kylie I slammed my little finger in excitement and nearly broke it. I was a fan anyway and already had ideas on how I would style her but she has her own ideas although she is open to suggestions.

'At the time she was becoming aware of fashion. We took her to her first fashion show in Paris. It was really exciting and we went to a Thierry Mugler show and a Jean Paul Gaultier show. The Gaultier show was really packed and the thing about Kylie is you always want to protect her. I basically picked her up, slung her over my shoulder and carried her through the crowd.'

David has had plenty of opportunity to see that famous Minogue determination close-up, and pays fulsome tribute to it. 'One word to sum up Kylie for me is tenacious. She works really hard and is a real trooper. But she also doesn't forget people. I hadn't seen her in a couple of years and out of the blue I got a call from her inviting me to her birthday.

'As for her bottom, it looks exactly the same as it has always done. She hasn't had anything done to it. As a stylist you do get to see a lot of people and I know Kylie's bum hasn't changed. Kylie is small but she is just in great proportion.'

'Kylie has been coming to our shop for quite a long time – about five years now,' says an assistant at VV Rouleaux. 'She is very unassuming and is absolutely minute. One time my husband was in the window dressing it and Kylie walked in – he just thought it was one of my 14-year-old daughter's school friends.

'Her bottom is not the first thing you notice about her,' she adds. 'It's her smile – she is so very bright and sparkly. Although she is very quiet and knows exactly what she wants, so we tend not to make too many suggestions.

'She's very interested in interiors and I get the impression she is quite involved in doing her own outfits. She loves our ribbons and she sews herself – she's very inventive.'

It seems no one who has come across la Minogue has a bad word to say about her. 'Kylie came to me in 2001 – I was recommended to her,' says Joseph Silvestre, a hairstylist at Ze in Chelsea. 'The first time she booked an appointment she used a different name. This woman came in, sat down and to be honest I didn't recognise her. But when she said "Hi I'm Kylie", I nearly died. We hit it off straight away and I did her hair all through the summer. She is wonderful as a client and as a person – very easy-going, relaxed and very easy to talk to. We talk about everything and anything – how work is going. She tells me what she is doing and we talk about the world. We'll go through OK! magazine just like anyone else.

'I've done her mum, Carol's hair,' Joseph adds. 'They are

very alike – both very down-to-earth – very normal. And although I haven't seen her for a few months I have been in touch. When she comes in she usually has her hair in a little bun and wears jeans and a T-shirt. I try not to have the salon over full but she never requests for it to be empty. Although people don't tend to bother her, on the odd occasion when someone has approached her she's been delighted to give her autograph. She usually comes to the salon on her own or with her assistant either in a car or she'll just walk down the road.

And that famous derrière? Joseph pronounces himself somewhat mystified about all the attention it's received of late: 'I don't know what the fuss is about her bottom – it is a lovely bottom but all this about her having implants is rubbish. It's so mean. I keep all the press cuttings so when Kylie comes in I ask her about some of the stories. Often she will say: "Oh I haven't read that", so I keep her up to date with what is being written about her. I think she reads some of what is written, though.

'As for her hair she is very good. She will leave it alone if she isn't doing anything – she is not one of these people who has her hair styled every day. She normally has lowlights or highlights keeping the underneath darkish – nothing that looks too artificial. But it all depends on what she is doing. Kylie is open to suggestions – she trusts me – but she knows what she likes and what she wants and of course I respect that.'

Despite the year-round bronzed glow, Kylie is extremely careful with her skin. She doesn't sunbathe, which is one of the reasons she is so enviably wrinkle free and is also a hangover from her Australian upbringing. Australians have been aware of the damage sun can wreak on the skin for much longer than the British (probably because they have so much more of it) and so Kylie covers up at all times. 'She never goes out without factor 30 sunscreen on – even in London,' says Carol Barnes. 'She screams at anyone she catches lying out in the sun.' Rather than bake herself to get a healthy colour, Kylie uses the St Tropez tan, also favoured by Victoria Beckham, topped up with Mac's golden bronze body powder.

But it's Will who remains the greatest influence on Kylie's look – and in describing it, he gives a revealing insight into Kylie's home life. Of her brief incarnation as a cowgirl he notes, 'That wasn't a really conscious thing, it just stemmed from the fact that she wears cowboy hats and tiaras around the house all the time so it seemed like fun, especially with the Gucci leather bikini. She loves shoes, she has thousands of pairs, but when she's shopping she loves vintage stuff and she'll pick up something brilliant for 10p and have it altered to fit her, rather than a Prada or Gucci.'

Will – who was once a theology student 'with no intention of becoming a priest' – is becoming as well known in his field as Kylie is in hers. He has also worked with Savage Garden, Tricky, Björk and Garbage and worked on projects for the magazines *Detour*, *Australian Vogue*, *The Face* and *Spin* but, very unusually for someone in his profession, does not see styling as the be-all and end-all of the world. 'I mean, I love it and working with Kylie is brilliant because you are involved in the whole process, but a lot of the time you are just a glorified courier,' he explains. 'Theology reminds me that there is more to life than clothes and fashion can kind of suck sometimes, it can be just crap.'

His friendship with Kylie isn't, though. 'If I've done anything for her over the last few years,' Will says, 'I hope I've given her some confidence in who she is and to stick up for herself, because she has incredible instincts. I hope I've also taught her to be a bit difficult sometimes, to put her foot down sometimes. My most consistent nag over the years is: trust yourself.'

Will says that one of Kylie's personality traits is insecurity. The woman herself agrees, but feels this is no bad thing. 'It's true for a lot of people, for a lot of performers,' she argues. 'It's something about performance, there is no right or wrong. There you are in front of an audience, and it's not accounting, where tables add up or they don't. [But] You obviously have room to manoeuvre and change and that's what I try to do.'

She has also finally come to terms with her frizzy-haired past. 'It's like anyone, when you look at old pictures of yourself and you cringe and ask, "How did I ever do that?"' she says. '"What was I thinking?" "What wasn't I thinking?"' And it was that – dare we say it – naffness in the early days that, Kylie believes, started her out as a gay icon. 'I think it was about 1989, when I was being given such a hard time in the press,' she muses. 'It was not a nice time for me, but I also remember people coming up to me in the street and rather than asking for something, they would give by saying things like, "Don't worry about what they write" or "We believe in you." It wasn't as if I was doing anything wrong, I wasn't hurting anyone or lying to them, but I was being attacked for being me. For being popular and being uncool. I feel that perhaps they [the gay community] reacted to that.'

Kylie was once asked what she considered to be her biggest fashion flop: 'Becoming famous in the late Eighties is a pretty good start – like being on *Top Of The Pops* in this brocade waistcoat and a low side ponytail and these huge earrings that were like bunches of grapes!' These days, she says, 'I love sparkle. I do like Dolce & Gabbana a lot – they're quite rock 'n' roll. I just like to sling a few things together. It took me years to work out my style.' And her favourite fashion item? 'Some pair of Manolo Blahnik shoes. And jeans – you can dress them up and dress them down.'

Age has not withered her, nor has custom staled her infinite variety. In fact now, approaching her mid-thirties, Kylie looks better than ever before. 'I'm not panicking yet,' she said towards the end of 2001. 'It's made me confident with my looks and image, finally. And I've come to accept that there are lots of different versions of me. Yes I love dressing up and being the showgirl but I also like bawling my eyes out like a six-year-old when things don't go right.'

Kylie is modest about being compared to Madonna. 'Madonna is the Queen of pop and I am the Princess,' she says. 'I'm content with that.' *Top Of The Pops Magazine* begged to differ. 'When it comes to pop, we really should address Kylie as Your Royal Highness!' it said. 'So let's roll out the red carpet and prepare for an audience with Her Majesty Minogue!' Will Baker has yet another take on it: 'She's not threatening, like Madonna,' he argues. 'She's not in your face, she's a girl next door and always will be. People feel a very personal connection with her and for a pop star that's quite hard to achieve.' Madonna has not publicly commented on comparisons between herself and the Australia's sexiest export, but her attitude to Kylie can be summed up by the fact that in 2001, she wore a T-shirt with Kylie's name emblazoned across it.

Kylie's looks and appeal might be the result of a lot of work on the part of a lot of people, but like all the truly great stars in this photographic age, a lot of her success is down to the fact that – quite simply – the camera loves her.

'In Kylie's case, she had a certain spark, that something extra,' Jan Russ, *Neighbours*' casting director, commented early on in Kylie's career. 'Also, she photographed beautifully. The camera adores her and she has this wonderful presence that comes through the camera lens. She has an extra charisma, or whatever you like to call it. It just comes through. You see her on camera and she has this wonderful something.'

Kylie attempts to lead as normal a life as she can. 'People who meet me for the first time often go, "How ya doin', Kyles?"' she says. 'And then you can see the horror spread over their faces when they realise they don't know you at all. You're not the person who lives down their street but they do know who you are. I do really ordinary things. I go down to Europa and walk home with my shopping bags, I go to the movies … people say to me, "Don't you have a bodyguard?" And I'm like, no? Pur-lease! It's a very Australian thing, I think. I remember when I moved to London ten years ago, it took me ages to get a cleaner because I had that attitude that you can't have something that someone else doesn't and you really shouldn't have someone clean up after you.'

Kylie is usually modest about her status as a sex symbol (although she did once announce, 'I don't try to be a sex bomb – I am one'). Asked in an interview on the MTV website in March how she feels about her poster adorning so many bedroom walls she said, 'I don't know how many walls I'm on. I'm sure I'm on a few dartboards as well. It's always a bit of give and take. Talking about myself as a pin-up or as a sex symbol or anything like that, that's a day job. "Her", she's gotta go and do it. I've got to deal with it when she comes home, in a state.

'I can talk a bit easier just having had these connections with people for many, many years. Back when they were kids and I was a young adult, so there must have been so many experiences that we've had together that I don't know about unless I meet these people and they tell me a story. But they're happening right now. Somewhere, someone's having an experience with the music or looking through a magazine. I find it very touching and very nice ... it humbles me, really. You know, it's no skin off my nose to sign something for them that's gonna make them happy, or their son, or their boyfriend or whoever.

'Maybe it's because over the years I've grown up in front of them. They've seen me do well, seen me fall, seen me making incredible blunders and embarrass-ments and I just think it makes for a strong and incredible relationship between them and myself. Years ago it was more frenzied when I would come to England, because *Neighbours* was on every single day and I was just thrust into the top fives of the chart all the time. I guess people thought, She might never come back, she's from a land so far away. But these days, it just seems like we're all a bit more grown up. They're used to me, feel like they know me, so perhaps they don't have to own me in the way that some other people might suffer. It's just like, "Hey Kyles, how're you doing?" It's nice.'

Well, it's nice most of the time, anyway. 'Some days I don't cope with it as well,' Kylie admits, though she adds hastily 'very infrequently. I've had an instant where I've been crying on a street, it was a long time ago, and I was standing with a boyfriend, and we must have been having a bit of a tiff, and I was in tears on the street. Someone came up to me in the middle of this saying, "Hi! You're Kylie Minogue! Can you sign this for me?" And I was just so ... taken aback. And there're the occasional times like that where I think, You're not treating me like a person ... This is not a sign of any manners whatsoever and I'm a bit old school when it comes to manners and stuff like that … But they know that I'm fragile sometimes.'

The other major influence on Kylie's career has been her manager, Terry Blamey. Terry has been with her from the very earliest days in 1987, after she had recorded 'Locomotion', but before it was released. At the time he was an agent, rather than manager and went on to look after other artists such as Dannii and Gina G, but these days he works for Kylie full time.

He now travels with her a great deal, which is unusual for a manager, looks after all aspects of her work, most importantly, 'keeping record companies in all corners of the earth on the case. They're employees and they're not as passionate about her. She's not their career, she's just their day job,' he explains.

Terry manages her to this day and, like Pete Waterman, is something of a father figure to Kyles. He has been a constant support, considering her IndieKylie phase not to have been a failure, simply not as successful as the rest of her career. She takes his advice; he has got her career back on track. He is one of the charmed inner circle that Kylie always listens to – if Kyle were a company rather than a person, Terry Blamey would be one of the chief directors of Kylie plc. Speaking of which …

14

Kylie

There are many advantages to being an internationally famous pop star and one of them is not having to worry too much about paying the bills. Kylie Minogue is a multi-millionairess many times over, estimated to be worth at least £16 million – and that's without taking into account her current breakthrough in the United States, which could earn her many millions more. Nor is this a recent development.

Kylie may be a glitter hippy in her appearance, but she's been anything but carefree in accumulating a fortune. She started making a lot of money very early on and has always been sensible with it. As long ago as 1990, she was turning down a tour that would have earned her £800,000 on the grounds that, 'I want to rest. Anyway, I don't need the money.'

And while Michael Hutchence might have taught Kylie about sex, art, wine, travel, poetry, drugs, very good hotels and I don't know what else, the teacher learned about one subject from his pupil: money. In 2002, five years after his death, it was revealed that Michael's fortune, if indeed it still exists, is proving remarkably difficult to track down given that it seems to be stashed away all over the world in various tax havens and trust funds. Michael learned how to look after his money from Kylie, just as she learned herself at the hands of an expert – her father, Ron.

Even from an early age Kylie's finances have been kept under strict control as Ron, an accountant, was leaving nothing to chance when he took responsibility for her growing fortune. Kylie once remarked that her father has always run her finances: telling her when to reign in her spending (which has never been excessive) and when it was all right to run wild.

And it was a fortune that was to grow and grow beyond their wildest expectations. In 1987 she was earning £150 a week starring in *Neighbours* – actually, not bad money back then for a school leaver – but when Kylie Ann Minogue joined the Stock, Aitken and Waterman stable back in the late Eighties she wasn't just on the road to becoming a star: she was on the fast track to making a fortune.

After the success of 'I Should Be So Lucky', Pete Waterman remembers: 'We released three more Kylie singles that year [1988] – 'Got To Be Certain', 'The Locomotion' (we'd worked on a new version from the one Duffy had engineered in Australia) and 'Je Ne Sais Pas Pourquoi', all of which went to number two, so within 12 months we'd made her a millionaire.' (This wasn't the only time Pete and co transformed someone's finances: in his autobiography, Pete wrote that he was second only to the Lottery in creating millionaires.)

And her fortune quickly grew from there: in 1989 she was said to have earned more than £7 million from her music and the film *The Delinquents*. Every year since then, even when her career appeared to be in decline, her wealth has increased, for her father has followed the most sensible line in investment and recommended that she diversify into property and shares – including a stake in the Fairfax Group, one of Australia's leading newspaper companies. The result is an international property portfolio in addition to investments in stocks, shares and high-earning insurance policies.

As far as one can tell, the future looks more rosy still. Kylie has finally broken into the American market: 'Can't Get You Out Of My Head' topped the dance chart, while her album *Fever* went in to the Billboard chart at number three. It was her first success in the States since 'The Locomotion' in 1987 and, according to industry insiders, could earn her a further $10 million. And guess what won America over?

'Kylie is the hottest property we've seen in a long time,' said one extremely overexcited source in the US record industry. 'But it's the body as much as the voice that has won us over – in particular that incredible tush. [That's American for bottom.] Her picture is everywhere. She's sassy in Tallahassee and has finer contours than the American hills.' Kylie herself is delighted by it all. 'I'm so used to being unknown in America that it's hard to believe this sudden change around. It feels fantastic.'

Not bad going for a little girl from Melbourne. But the sudden accumulation of wealth was not going to change Kylie: not for her the stories of instant excess and a dwindling fortune – and even when she started behaving like a rock chick a couple of years later, she remained financially astute. Right from the start, under the watchful gaze of her father Ron, Kylie had her financial dealings taken care of. In 1989, despite having already earned more by the age of 22 than most people will throughout the whole of their lifetime, Kylie insisted on living on £110 a week – all the while making sure her growing fortune was carefully stashed away for the future.

Her management team were also working on her behalf behind the scenes: in 1989, they hammered out a new deal for Kylie to guarantee that she got a minimum of 10 per cent royalties from worldwide record deals. Given the fact that she had by now topped the charts in 23 countries, it was an astute move to make.

Property was the first and most obvious investment to be made and has been a feature of Kylie's saving and investment right from the start. In 1989, she bought a Victorian house in Melbourne for £250,000, spending a further £300,000 on renovations for the property, which dated back to 1880. 'It's very old for Australia, but I just love it,' she said at the time. But she didn't immediately move in. 'I haven't got time at the moment, so I'm staying with my parents until the decoration has been completed,' she went on (she was also spending an awful lot of time with Jason Donovan, who owned a property nearby).

'But it's a beautiful Victorian house. I'm going to have it extended and renovated and all done in period. Although it has got a wonderful Seventies bathroom and kitchen, I'm taking them out and having it all original. I want it to look just like a Victorian home inside and out. I love that era and hate most modern-style houses.'

Kylie's next brush with the property market came the following year: she was offered a luxury home near Tokyo worth £250,000 for three days' work – her first Japanese tour. The deal was said to have had beneficial tax implications if she took the property rather than cash, although it was unclear what she eventually chose to do. The following year, having moved to England, Kylie bought a three-bedroom flat in Chelsea for £300,000 – and even the most conservative estimates would value it at very significantly more today.

It emerged at the time, incidentally, that Kylie still hadn't moved into her first house: 'A few years ago I bought a house in Melbourne,' she said a few years after purchasing that Victorian property, 'but it's still not finished because I wanted to do it just right and I never have enough time.' Exactly the same was to be the case in Chelsea: Kylie lived in a hotel for some months before finally moving in to her new bachelor girl pad.

Nor were Kylie's earnings just coming from her acting and singing careers. She's never gone over the top doing promotional work, but she has done advertisements here and there – work that also stems back over many years. As far back as 1990, she was believed to have earned around £750,000 for participating in a commercial campaign for Coca Cola in Australia: it featured a pizza delivery boy going up to a penthouse flat while whistling his favourite song by Kylie Minogue. And guess who answers the door?

Fellow Coke promoters at the time included George Michael, Don Johnson and New Kids On The Block and Coke went on to sponsor Kylie's 1991 'Rhythm of Love' tour. By this time she could also command more than £10,000 for public appearances, placing her firmly in the big league of A-list stars who can very nearly name their own fees.

Of course, in the years since then, Kylie's earnings have continued to rocket through records and concerts, with her early success more than enough to cushion her through a difficult patch: between 1988 and 1992, Kylie notched up 14 top five hits, bringing in millions in the process. She also has her own company, Kaydeebee, which owns the copyright on her photographs, merchandise and music. This means that whenever you hear a Kylie record being played or see a Kylie-commissioned photograph in a newspaper or magazine, she is almost certain to be getting a chunk of the profits.

Kylie's protective about the use of her name, too. In 2001 she sued the Australian magazine *Cleo* over an article in which it claimed she had endorsed Tommy's Girl perfume: entitled 'Tommy's Girl Rocks Kylie', the article said the fragrance was created for her. This was not the case and Kylie forced a settlement with Cleo's parent company ACP. Kylie cultivates a very charming, hippyish persona, often claiming that she hardly knows what she'll be doing from one week to the next, but it is increasingly clear that she's inherited her father's business acumen and will protect, as well as promote, the Kylie 'brand' as she sees fit.

And while Kylie may have had hits and misses with records throughout the years, that Kylie brand is as strong as ever. In fact, in recent years she seems to have done a lot more promotional work than previously, possibly aware that she has a shelf life as an artist – although it's proving to be a pretty long one – and should make the most of it while she can. She's been careful not to make the same mistake as people such as the Spice Girls, though, who went too far in the early days and promoted everything they could lay their hands on (or so it sometimes seemed), thus resulting in massive overexposure. Kylie has picked products carefully, judging the effect they will have on her image and whether they will fit in with the Kylie brand. Thus we have seen her advertising an awful lot of lingerie, as well as soft drinks, international travel and a sexy little sports car. It's not just a good way to make a lot of money; it's also a good way to promote her own image.

The biggest deal came in 2001, when Kylie switched allegiance from Coke to Pepsi, landing a £2.5-million contract to advertise the soft drink Down Under. But unlike some of the other advertisements Kylie was to make that year, of which more below, these ads were to feature a fully dressed

Minogue: 'Ours is a fine, upstanding brand,' sniffed a Pepsi spokesman. 'We do not encourage our artists to remove their clothes.' Again, Kylie was in good company: fellow Pepsi stars included Britney Spears, Madonna, Michael Jackson and the Spice Girls before they went too far. And because of its roster of artists, Pepsi is seen as a good drink for a performer to advertise: there is a certain prestige in signing up with one of the world's most famous names.

Kylie has put the money to good use; her lifestyle has never been excessive. As we have seen, she loves designer clothes, but is equally likely to splash out on second-hand clothes – such as that pair of gold hot pants. (And her reaction to the £50,000 offer for them is telling as well: she immediately mused on what a good investment she'd made rather than relating them to her own sex appeal.) And as for her designer wardrobe – Sting once remarked that when you're rich, you never have to pay for anything, especially your clothes so it's a fair bet that Kylie, at the very least, gets offered good discounts when she goes on the odd shopping spree.

Clothing generally has been good to Kylie. In 1998, she joined the likes of Claudia Schiffer, Helena Christensen, Naomi Campbell and Jade Jagger, when she was photographed by Ellen von Unworth for H&M Hennes. The photographs, which concentrated on Kylie in her undies, were a great success and a picture of them plastered all over the underground actually features in Kylie's coffee table book.

In 2001, a further commercial opportunity became available when she designed her own range of lingerie called Love Kylie x, which was launched first in Australia and then in the UK. Even the *Guardian*, not normally the kind of newspaper to celebrate Kylie's commercial exploits, was delighted, calling the product 'Magic!'

The manufacturer issued the following breathless statement at launch: 'Holeproof is proud to launch the best thing in lingerie for years – Love Kylie x. Personally designed by Australia's own Kylie Minogue, Love Kylie x is a reflection of that distinctive Kylie style – sexy but still "girl next door", pert and provocative but stylish and sophisticated. The Love Kylie x collection has been designed to maximise style and comfort and includes a range of briefs, bras and camis.' Hyperbole, yes, but backed up by the underwear itself. The only trouble is that it doesn't make anyone else look like Kylie. As Cathy Dennis, who wrote 'Can't Get You Out Of My Head' once remarked, 'I wish I looked like Kylie when I take my clothes off. Respect.'

Kylie took her raunchy image to new extremes in the same year when she made an advertisement for Agent Provocateur, which makes very sexy, very expensive underwear. She donated her £150,000 fee to charity but certainly made cinema-goers sit up and take notice. The ad was so over the top it wasn't shown on television and only appeared in cinemas for films rated 18. It featured Kylie in bra and knickers riding a bucking bronco: 'I was flattered when they asked me to star in the ad,' said Kylie, 'and I loved doing it. It was sexy and fun.' An Agent Provocateur spokeswoman added, 'This is our first cinema advert and it's very exciting and sexy. People will be queuing to see Kylie. She's amazing.'

In an interview, Kylie admitted that the ad was really pretty outrageous 'Oh my God!' she cried. 'I've really outdone myself this time! I'm basically riding a velvet bronco, wearing black lace knickers, bra, suspenders, stockings, high heels and a slight … sweaty glow. I was pulling all these manoeuvres and my make-up artist, Caroline, didn't know where to look. She said, "How do you do that? In front of everyone?"

'And I said, "How can I get up and do a lot of the things I do? I just do it." You could put anyone in the same get-up doing the same moves and they may not get away with it. It's because people know me so well – or even if they don't, there's something in the way I am. It's like I'm winking but I'm not winking.' The catchline of the advertisement, incidentally, is: 'Would all the men please stand up.'

Another of Kylie's property investments is in Paris: she still owns a flat in the French capital as a hangover from her time with Stephane, which she escapes to from time to time because she can be 'invisible' there. 'Paris is great because I can sit in a café and watch the world go by,' she once confided. 'It is nice being an observer for once rather than one of the observed.'

Appropriately, given her love of Paris, she has appeared in advertisements for Eurostar, replacing the American actor John Malkovich. The ad showed Kylie taking the train for a shopping spree and she is glimpsed running across bridges, dissolving into crowds, sipping coffee in cafes and trying on a wedding dress: 'Kylie is one of the biggest pop icons of the moment, but she's still approachable. She's perfect for the company,' enthused a spokesman.

The ads – which were shown in the break in *Coronation Street*, one of the prime time slots for an advertisement to be aired – appeared just before 'Can't Get You Out Of My Head' reached the top of the charts and Joanna Howard, marketing manager at Eurostar commented, 'The commercial has a special feel because of Kylie's very natural expression of liberation and excitement.' Kylie earned an estimated £200,000 for the £2-million campaign – and its timing did her new single no harm at all.

As you might expect by now, Kylie isn't interested in simply hoarding all that money she makes. For one thing, she is extremely generous to her parents. In January 2002, she bought a £1 million home for Ron and Carol in Monmouth Avenue, Canterbury, one of the most prestigious streets in Melbourne. A 1940s, two-storey construction, it has a heated swimming pool and tennis court. Ron, who was 60 when the house was bought, had been ill and so the property was seen as a combination of a Christmas, thank you and get well present: 'She owes much of her wealth to her dad's judgement,' explained a friend.

And Kylie has also been investing in more property in Britain: in early 2002, she bought a £400,000 flat in Shoreditch, the new art capital of London, which for a while she shared with James, before returning to Chelsea. It was a two-bedroom waterside luxury loft conversion with wooden floors, situated close to the Bricklayers Arms pub – like Madonna, Kylie had become an unlikely aficionado of Britain's public houses.

And her promotional work continues. Most recently she signed up with Ford to promote the Street Ka, a little 1.6 litre two-seater that will retail for £11,000. Kylie will dance provocatively around it as well as draping herself on the bonnet – 'They are the perfect match, both small and very sexy,' said a Ford spokeswoman; the company will also sponsor Kylie's 2002 concert tour.

So Kylie has yet another persona: one that has yet to make it into her videos, but one that is quite as important as the rest: TycoonKylie. She has learned at first hand that she works in a very rough and fickle industry, and although James claims that she'll still be wearing her gold hot pants at the age of 70, it's unlikely that people would pay quite so much to see them.

Like the wise little daughter of an accountant that she is,

KYLIE

Kylie has put something aside for a rainy day – such a significant something, in fact, that she need never work again. It is a very pleasant situation for a 34-year-old to be in and is proof positive that Kylie works because she wants to, not because she has to.

And anyway, what else would she do if she wasn't working any more? 'I don't know how I would react,' said Kylie in an interview, when asked that question. 'Because it takes so long to get used to this kind of life. I love making videos, I like performing. Whether it's a photo shoot, making videos or meeting kids in hospital, I really love working. Oh God, I sound like a beauty contestant, don't I? "I like pets!"'

Kylie was also once asked if she ever thought about what she would have been doing had fate not led her into show business. 'I do think about it, but I don't think about it for too long,' she admitted. 'When I was at school, I thought I might go to business school, so I sometimes wonder what I'd be like if I worked in an office. You know, Kylie the office girl. I reckon I wouldn't be any different, you know, I'd still be me. I'd still be a performer wherever I was.' And very probably a rich performer, too.

15

Comeback Kylie

In the early years of the new century, Kylie's life seemed to be firmly back on track. She herself coined the phrase 'Comeback Kylie,' and was for the moment, happily ensconced with James. None other than Madonna recognised this when she wore a t-shirt emblazoned with Kylie's name – Kylie herself was flabbergasted. 'Here was this icon,' she said. 'I mean, I was like every other teenager, putting on a million belts and lace gloves – and to see my name on her t-shirt was surreal, it was great. I've only ever met her at the MTV awards where she wore the t-shirt. The first thing I think I said was, "Hi! Nice to meet you." She asked me if I liked the t-shirt and I said, "Yes, I do like the t-shirt, thank you."' Later she was more pragmatic, musing on what would be the cost of advertising her name on the most widely viewed billboard in the world.

This was also the year in which she was happiest with James, who she had met at the 2000 Brit Awards. James was a successful model in his own right, starring in the Peugeot 206 and L'Oreal advertisements and initially it seemed that this might be the one to last. 'It's very sweet and I don't want to put any pressure on it,' said Kylie firmly when asked about her new beau. 'I've felt in the past that I've been searching for something and I haven't been able to find it. I've had times when I've said to my girlfriends, 'Oh, you've all got boyfriends and I haven't.'

Initially the omens were good. Kylie called James her 'delightful scruff from Essex,' and said he treated her like a princess. That he was seven years her junior didn't seem to be an issue, as with any couple, the two met one another's parents and visited each other's earliest homes, much to the bemusement of some of James's friends. One bumped into the couple in November 2001 and was taken aback when he discovered who James's new girlfriend was. 'When I saw him, they'd just been bowling and seemed really happy,' he said.

'I didn't know who the woman on his arm was but he introduced her as Kylie. I nearly fell through the floor when I discovered it was *the* Kylie. We were all gobsmacked when we found out he was going out with her. It's really strange because he fancied her for about 14 years. Everyone remembers how smitten he was with her at school. Teachers would even sing the Dolly Parton hit 'Jolene' to him but changed the words to 'Charlene' after her character in Neighbours. James was always a good laugh about it, though and never got upset. He had pictures of her up in his bedroom and never missed Neighbours. Now he's got her in his bed, the lucky sod.'

But this might well provide a clue as to why the relationship didn't last. After one of their mini-bust ups before the final break, James actually denied having Kylie's picture up on his wall as a schoolboy: it might have been by that time he had tired of being the very much less famous half of a celebrity couple. Indeed, he also spoke about the strains placed on a relationship when one part of it is as famous as Kylie. Like so many men, it seemed he simply couldn't cope with the fact that his girlfriend was on the receiving end of so much more attention than him.

Kylie and James moved into a flat in London's cutting edge Clerkenwell district, but despite her new found happiness, Kylie was clearly determined to never again let her career falter as it had done some years earlier. The round of work continued to be never-ending and she continued to go from strength to strength, with the latest accolade coming in the form of a second Kylie waxwork at Madame Tussauds. The waxwork raised some eyebrows, not least from the lady herself, given that it had her on her hands and knees, with the famous bottom rising into the air, clad only in a basque and knickers. Indeed, it was widely held to be vulgar, not the impression Kylie or Madame Tussauds wished to convey, and so after some deliberation it was covered in the much longer black dress worn by the original. Kylie was greatly relieved. 'As for my waxwork at Madame Tussauds, let's just say I was a little surprised at the slight lack of wardrobe judgment,' she said.

For a while, though, Kylie's relationship with James seemed serious. When she appeared on *Parkinson* in February 2002, Parky asked if she was ready to get married and have children. 'I think so – yes,' she said. 'I always try not to say yes or no because who knows? But I'm sure it will happen. My career has been the most important thing for a long, long time.'

Her career was going stunningly well. In September 2001 another challenge had been overcome; she went head to head in the charts with Victoria Beckham, who was releasing her first solo single, 'Not Such An Innocent Girl.' Kylie, meanwhile, was about to release, 'Can't Get You Out Of My

Head,' written by Cathy Dennis and Rob Davies. Billed as the 'battle of the babes,' the media was greatly entertained by the coincidence that both records were to be released on the same date. Kylie was cautious. 'As soon as I saw we had the same release date, I thought, hmmm, has anybody thought about changing the schedule?' she admitted. 'I knew there would be a media frenzy if we stuck with that date.' In the event she had nothing to worry about, 'Can't Get You Out Of My Head' went straight in at number one, her thirty-fifth single in the top 20, ultimately selling 306,000.

In acknowledgement of her status as superstar-cum-national treasure, Kylie was awarded her own show, An Audience With Kylie Minogue, which featured such luminaries as Julian Clary, Boy George, Melinda Messenger, both Minogue siblings and Kermit the Frog, with whom she sang 'Especially For You.' She also put in an acclaimed performance as the Absinthe Fairy in the film *Moulin Rouge*.

But it was a heavy workload and the relationship also entailed long absences. In mid 2002, Kylie went on a highly successful world tour, the Fever tour, culminating in her native Australia. And it was there, when playing in Sydney, that she had a reunion with Kell Hutchence, Michael's father. The first great love of her life was still clearly on her mind. Kylie had sent Kell and his second wife Susie tickets to the show. Afterwards, they went backstage to see her in her dressing room. 'It was an emotional moment,' said Kell. 'There alone with a cup of tea sat Kylie. She was sitting there quietly in her robe, pretty exhausted from the show but just glowing.'

'She was very gracious and just the same sweet girl I remembered, so friendly and good natured. You couldn't meet a more unpretentious and normal person. It's so easy to see why Michael loved her. I kept thinking, 'If only Michael could see her now.' I congratulated her on her wonderful performance and she mentioned Michael. We spoke quite a lot about him, reminisced a little about the past, but I want to keep those things private. She did tell me though that when she did her show at Wembley Stadium, she was thinking of Michael and his performance there.' What James Gooding made of the fact that Kylie still seemingly considered Michael to be the great love of her life is not something he would want to discuss, but it is unlikely to have gone down well. Even so, the two managed a brief break in Bali at the end of the tour.

Nor was she any more prepared to put her career on hold for him than she had been for any of her other boyfriends. As she prepared the release of a new single, 'Come Into My World', she won her first major US award, the MTV Video Music award for Best Choreography for 'Can't Get You Out Of My Head'. She then immediately flew off to Paris to film the video that went with her new release, a punishing work schedule for anyone, and so it is perhaps not surprising that in September 2002, rumours first began to circulate of both a break-up with James and some sort of nervous collapse. What is certain is that Kylie flew back to Australia for a few weeks holiday with her mother.

Certainly everyone was keen to play down suggestions that Kylie was in any way unwell. 'She's been working really hard and she's having a holiday with her mum,' snapped a spokeswoman for Kylie's Australian record label, Festival-Mushroom Records. 'What she does on her holidays is none of her record company's business.' Dannii Minogue was equally clear that Kylie was perfectly well. 'Kylie has not had a nervous breakdown,' she said. 'She has been working round the clock for three years and who can blame her for taking a short break. She decided to go to a remote part of Oz because she wanted to spend quality time with our mum without any hassle.'

But Dannii also revealed something else – that the rumours of a split with James were turning out, temporarily at least, to be true. 'Kylie has had a lot of ups and downs this year,' she said. 'James has been one of the downs. Obviously she's been very upset about splitting up as they had been together for a long time. But marrying James was never on Kylie's list of priorities. And neither was having kids with him. She's not worried about her biological clock ticking. She's still a young woman and will have kids when the time is right.'

Kylie herself finally spoke out. 'I'm fine, I'm fine, I'm more than ok,' she said in response to questions about her health. 'I am single and I must say I haven't been out, just spending time with my family. Just being, which is normally the hardest thing for me to do. So I haven't really felt single or not single. I've just been being me.'

In actual fact, this was by no means the end of the relationship. Kylie and James did not break off contact. Indeed, they continued to see one another regularly when they could. After that break with her mother, Kylie was back on form and ending 2002 with as much energy as it had begun. Her schedule was more frenetic than ever: a greatest hits compilation; appearances on the London stage in *The Play What I Wrote* and the Royal Variety Performance; more awards from MTV Europe for Best Pop Act and Best Dance Act and plans to make more appearances in the United States. Something had to give in her relationship with James, and it did.

The final split, when it came, was a bitter one. Indeed, the signs were there that there were problems from the start. The pair had been pictured arguing on numerous occasions both before and after the initial break and matters were not helped when James was photographed with Sophie Dahl and the socialite Beverley Bloom. It was also apparent James had a roving eye. 'They are always rowing,' Michael Edwards-Hammond, Dannii's old boyfriend, said as far back as 2001. 'It's partly from jealousy on both sides. James is still a bit of a boy and has a real eye for the ladies. He can't help flirting and it gets Kylie's back up. And he doesn't like the inevitable attention she gets from men.'

It was this jealousy that was to provide a spectacular bust-up. By February 2003 Kylie was ready for yet another venture. Her lingerie range, Love Kylie was launched in the UK after a successful start in Australia, with Kylie explaining she was very involved in all aspects of the line. 'I've always had that since day one, starting first as an actress, "Oh, you can't sing, you can't do that, you can't do this,"' she said. 'I'm so used to confronting the pigeonholes. I've battled against that for a long time and quite successfully. Now I think people expect different things from me. I don't know quite how I did it but I am pleased.'

But on her return to the UK, while her professional life was running smoothly, her personal life was not. James had been brooding about the split, becoming, according to some friends, utterly obsessed with his ex. And in fact, it rapidly turned into the nastiest break-up Kylie had ever had. Despite the fact that he was soon to reveal the full extent of his own infidelity, James had become increasingly angry with Kylie and found it impossible to move on. Shortly after the split he was upset by reports linking her to Jamiroquai singer Jay Kay, but that was nothing compared to his behaviour at and after the Brit Awards held in February 2003.

The problem could be summed up in two words: Justin

Timberlake. The story of what happened that night was to go down as one of the most notorious episodes in Kylie's career. The US singer performed a duet with Kylie at the awards, at one point grabbing the world's most famous bottom as they danced. Kylie clearly didn't object and Justin went on to wax lyrical on the subject: 'On a scale of one to 10, Kylie's bum is 58,' he announced, later adding, 'I hear everyone in this country is obsessed with Kylie's bum. I can see why – now I'm obsessed with it too.' Kylie was equally pleased by her dancing partner. 'I've fancied him for a while,' she confided to a friend. 'He's a great mover.'

Unfortunately James was in the audience and was enraged by what he saw on stage. 'Yeah, I really enjoyed it tonight,' he snarled to onlookers. 'That really made the performance for me – it was the best bit.' Alarmed by his increasingly aggressive behaviour, Kylie told her management to keep James away from her and slipped off to dinner at the Montpelliano restaurant in Knightsbridge, with her sister Dannii, Janet Jackson – and Justin.

The quartet then went on to the Sanderson Hotel for a party held by EMI. It was then that the drama really began: James managed to sneak in and launched into a screaming fit at Kylie, accusing her of making a mockery of him and demanding to know the truth about Jay Kay. At first, Kylie tried to calm the situation down, introducing him to Justin and trying to be polite. But the extremely drunk James would not be placated and soon began yelling and shouting again. Clearly shocked, Kylie and Dannii tried to leave, only to have a furious James block their path, shouting at them, before security guards finally got him under control.

'Kylie smiled, trying to keep calm and not to be seen to have a row in public, but James wouldn't let up,' said an onlooker. 'As Kylie went to walk out, James stepped in the way and two security men stepped in and held him back as she left.' Kylie herself didn't manage to keep cool, 'I don't want James anywhere near me,' she yelled to one of the guards as she passed. 'Keep him fucking away from me. I don't want him getting in my car. Get me out of here now.'

After this, the night assumed an element of farce. A furious Kylie drove off in one car; meanwhile Justin, Dannii and Dannii's friend Ben went off in another. And indeed, Dannii's presence was an effective smokescreen: the next morning rumours flew around the music business to the effect that she had spent the night with Justin Timberlake. It was only some weeks later that it emerged through the press that the lucky girl was none other than Kylie, who sneaked off at 6am the following morning. Dannii later confessed, 'Ben and I dropped Justin off at the hotel and went home and didn't go inside the hotel.'

Justin was coy when asked about it later. He admitted to the paper, 'She came in late and we had some drinks. She was upset about her argument with James Gooding and I was there to look after her. Kylie's very cool and such an intelligent, gorgeous woman. It was a great night at the Brits. Kylie was truly out of this world. We were at the EMI party afterwards and were all just hanging out and drinking. Then all this commotion happened with Kylie and James, so I gave her sister Dannii a lift. But she didn't want to come into the hotel for a drink and I went in alone. Then I got a call from Kylie and I said come to the hotel and have a drink. That's all I wanna say on the matter.'

In fact, there was one suggestion as to what had happened by Greg Brennan, the celebrity photographer. 'Kylie's car eventually pulled up to the Mandarin and Mike Moorcroft, who looks after the UK end of security for all American stars, came out and escorted her and her personal assistant inside,' he said. 'He put his arm around Kylie and shielded her from anyone watching, but I know it was Kylie because I know what car she had that night. All three of them ran in and around five to ten minutes later the PA woman came out again, jumped into the car which was still outside and drove off. Kylie was in the hotel and left about 6am – by the back way.'

Nor was that the end of the Kylie/Justin flirtation. A little while later, both were due to appear at the Grammy Awards in New York, where they again performed together. 'She's a great mover and we had a great time at the Grammys last week too,' said the gallant Justin afterwards. He had to leave for Los Angeles the next day, at which point Kylie cancelled her plans to stay in New York for a week and went on to LA, too. 'She was due to stay in New York and cleared her diary,' said a source in the *News of the World* article. 'But mysteriously she got on a flight to LA with her PA. She and Justin have been in contact and met up at her hotel.' The hotel in question was the Chateau Marmont and it was a fortuitous choice, for it was there that she bumped into a rising French actor˘

Meanwhile, returning to the Brits evening, James was still continuing to cause trouble. After being set free by the security guards at The Sanderson, he headed to Kylie's flat in Chelsea, continuing to scream and bang on the door before calling her on her mobile. A passerby actually heard his half of the call: 'It seemed she was saying she was inside the house,' he revealed. James could be clearly heard on the street: 'Where are you?' he said. 'You're lying, you're not at home, I'm outside. Tell me where you are ˘ You're lying.'

The following morning, once he'd sobered up, James was appalled by his own actions and tried for one last reconciliation with Kylie. 'He's knows he's made a fool of himself and that drink had a lot to do with it,' Amelia Trowbridge, a friend of his revealed. 'But he'll knock that on the head if Kylie will come back. He's been on the phone to her constantly. He's just pleading with her to take him back.' But Kylie had finally had enough – which led James to attempt a terrible revenge.

He sold his story to the *News Of The World*, the first of Kylie's boyfriends ever to do so, lashing out and flinging insults in a torrent of fury and upset. 'The Kylie the British public knows is the cheeky, chirpy Aussie, loaded with talent and buckets of sex appeal,' he began. 'And that's the Kylie I fell in love with. Who wouldn't? But she turned into a self-obsessed, virtually friendless control freak, desperate to pursue her own ambitions as far as she could take them. None of the public saw that side of her and even I was stunned by the full force of her selfishness.'

James went on to claim he and Kylie had slept together shortly before the night of the Brits and as if that were not enough, he bitterly predicted that Kylie would end up as a lonely old spinster, with only a cat by her side. He was also keen to put his side of the story about that night at the Brits. 'That night was the final straw in our relationship,' said James. 'After their performance Kylie was sitting opposite Justin when I went up and said, 'Hi.' She was very standoffish. I asked her, 'Do you fancy a drink?' She rudely snapped, 'No.' It was clear she felt being seen with a big American pop star like Justin was far more important than our friendship.'

News of his own infidelities with, amongst others, Sophie

Dahl and Martine McCutcheon followed, as James revealed that the problems had begun in 2001. Kylie was about to go off on a three month tour and James asked if it was ok to date other women: Kylie was 'not thrilled,' he went on, but said she'd understand. There followed a series of splits, culminating in the Brit Awards, which had upset James so much, he said, that he'd taken an overdose. He had gone to a friend's house and taken champagne and cocaine, before going home. When he woke up, he revealed, he took an overdose of Temazepam tranquillisers and downed half a bottle of Jack Daniels. And, he claimed that it was all Kylie's fault. 'I'd let her get inside my head and she'd rejected me,' said James said in the *News of the World*. 'I felt on the verge of a breakdown.'

Nothing like this had ever happened to Kylie before. She was devastated by the betrayal and if James had thought this was a way of pushing her back into his life, he was wrong. 'This is the end for James,' said a friend of Kylie's. 'Kylie will cut him out of her life for good. He will be airbrushed from her history. As far as she is concerned, that's it. Kylie hoped they would be able to stay friends when their relationship finished but James has made sure it will never happen.' And indeed, that was the absolute end of anything between the two.

James, meanwhile, was widely condemned for his actions, not least by his own father. 'He has been playing the field and has had armfuls of girls, all high profile types,' snapped David Gooding, an erstwhile advertising executive who now ran a pub in Scotland. 'He even told Kylie about his affair with Sophie Dahl, so what did he expect? James is not a drinker, and as far as I know doesn't do drugs. He is quoted as saying he was making a cry for help. Naturally you feel sorry for anyone who does this. But James is 27 and is a man of the world and I am sure he will be all right. And he is bound to have received a tidy sum for the story.' But there was already something else in Kylie's life to soften the blow. His name was Olivier Martinez.

Kylie and Olivier had first met shortly before-hand in the lobby of a Los Angeles hotel in March 2003. There has been speculation that all is not well within that romance either, but at the time Olivier was clearly the man to deal with the hurt James had caused. Asked some time later if James's revelations had made it hard for her to have faith in a new partner, Kylie replied, 'It wasn't really difficult to trust a man again, but I can only think about Olivier in answer to that. It was easy to trust him.'

Olivier Martinez, sometimes known as the 'French Brad Pitt,' is a major star in his own right. Originally from a working class background, he was brought up in one of the less well off areas of Paris, initially following his boxer father into the ring. He left school young, with no qualifications, and drifted from one job to the next until he entered acting school aged 23. Success came almost immediately as he started to appear on French television, before moving into film and starring in, amidst much else, *Unfaithful*, with Richard Gere. Unlike James Gooding, he was becoming as well known as Kylie herself – and unlike James Gooding, he was not prone to moodiness. The world was instantly agog. Could this, finally, be 'The One'?

Certainly, once outed as a couple, the pair were more than happy to be seen together everywhere. This was not, after all, Kylie's first relationship with a Frenchman and she was pleased to spend time in Paris, the city she had got to know through her previous romance. Olivier's influence became clear in other ways, as well. Kylie's look began to change; the miniskirts began to disappear, while a Bardo-esque series of pictures made an appearance in one photoshoot.

Kylie began covering up, she was even pictured wearing Chanel – albeit slightly skimpy Chanel – while at the same time cutting back on work commitments and even, for the first time in a long time, sitting down to a regular daily breakfast. 'It's chocolate croissants nearly every morning, and feeling happy and taking time,' said a bemused sounding Kylie. 'Having managed to actually live some life and it works. The world doesn't cave in. It's amazing.' There was early - yet inaccurate - speculation that she was pregnant. It seemed that nothing could go wrong.

But, as so often in Kylie's love life, strains began to show almost immediately. Kylie, as ever, had no intention of putting her career on the backburner to pursue a relationship, while Olivier is a working actor with his own life to build. And so, after an all too brief honeymoon period, rumours surfaced that all was not well. In Canada at a baseball game, Olivier was pictured holding hands with his co-star Angelina Jolie in the film *Taking Lives*. Kylie actually flew out to Canada to see him once the Jolie pictures appeared, both insisted afterwards that the visit had been long planned and that nothing was wrong. Indeed, she was irritable about it. 'It was very annoying,' Kylie said afterwards. 'When I arrived in Montreal, he was actually at the baseball game. So the whole story about, "She's seen the picture of him so she's flown over," I mean, even if it had happened – how the hell do they know what two people said when they were alone in a trailer?'

But whether or not there had been problems, Olivier's influence continued to be felt. Throughout 2003 Kylie was working on a new album, *Body Language*, and for perhaps the first time in her entire career did not go on tour to support it when it was released at the end of the year. Clearly his advice to let up on the workload a little had been heeded, to say nothing of the fact that Kylie did not want to start suffering from nervous exhaustion again. And the change of image continued. Kylie-watchers observed that her look was becoming more languorous while at the same time, to the chagrin of her male admirers, she continued to cover up. Talking about what to wear to promote the new album, Kylie said firmly that, 'I'm not going to be in a bathing suit. We've tried to move away from flesh. We realised that the flesh thing is everywhere now, everywhere. And I think it's important to differentiate.' And was she keen to keep some flesh covered just for herself? 'Yes,' said Kylie firmly. 'And for my boyfriend.'

She was even tiring of the continuing fascination in the world's most famous bottom. 'I'm partly flattered by it but over a certain point ... The Bottom,' she said. 'Well, that did spiral somewhat out of control. But in the end, it's a laugh, and I'd be feeling a lot worse if it was like, errgh, look at that!'

Will Baker, Kylie's stylist and the most important person when it comes to her image, agreed. 'What an impact those hot pants made,' he said. 'But I want to take her away from the sex symbol thing now. She loves French sophistication and I think it's perfect for her – especially as she's with Olivier, a French movie star. We spent three days shopping in Paris recently. We didn't even go out in the evenings as we were so busy having appointments all day. Shopping has become increasingly difficult for Kylie – it's not unlike a military operation.'

Kylie was at the end of some teasing about all of this, given the amount of flesh she'd revealed in the past, but she and Will were aware of the fact that she was approaching her late 30s, and simply had to change her look. But while Kylie might have been getting tired of The Bottom, the public clearly wasn't. In June 2003 the Brighton-based artist Simon Etheridge put an almost lifesize picture of Kylie in her gold hot pants in the window of his Art Asylum gallery. This immediately caused traffic hold-ups as motorists slowed down to have a proper look.

'People have been a bit frustrated because as they drive past, they see it and slow down,' he revealed. 'It's a narrow street and one-way so people are hitting their horns. It's caused some amusement for us in the gallery but not for the motorists.' The painting itself eventually sold for £895.

16

Kylie – Queen of Pop

Kylie certainly remained popular in all quarters. In June 2003, she was the surprise star guest at Boy George's birthday party in Ronnie Scott's, turning up to sing 'Happy Birthday' in a turquoise mini-dress. The Boy proclaimed himself 'star struck'. British Airways clearly felt the same and signed her up as an ambassador to launch their Tropical Beaches brochure 2004.

There was a small blip in her career when two of her films, *Streetfighter* and *Bio-Dome*, featured in a poll of the hundred worst films of all time, but, given that Kylie herself had declared that they had been a mistake, none of her entourage was unduly alarmed.

A bigger blip, although it had nothing do to with the lady herself, came in July 2003, after a television crew faked her kidnap. Concerned neighbours called the police after witnessing someone who turned out to be a Kylie lookalike being shoved into a car outside the singer's Chelsea flat. It later turned out that Channel 4 were involved.

'The abduction scene was filmed to illustrate the crazy

KYLIE: STORY OF A SURVIVOR

lengths some people will go to to get close to a celebrity,' said a clearly embarrassed spokeswoman. 'It's most unfortunate that the lookalike did turn out to be too much of a lookalike and caused distress.' The lookalike herself, Faye Richards, who is, in fact, distantly related to Kylie, was also not too pleased.

'It wasn't made clear to her what was going to happen,' said a friend. 'Faye said she didn't like the thought of it from the start, but by the time she got there it was too late to stop anything. Faye has met Kylie many times and feels appalled that she was involved in anything that would put her in danger. Apparently, Kylie had left her flat just five minutes before the kidnap.'

Kylie herself was, understandably, livid. 'I thought it was a really stupid thing for a TV crew to do,' she said. 'I was really surprised when I heard. I think they did act irresponsibly.'

And her new strategy of covering up was paying off. James Gooding once remarked that when she was a grandmother she would still be wearing hot pants, but Kylie herself clearly realised that as she got older, like Madonna, she was going to have to cultivate an image based not solely on appearance. A joke 'Ban the Bum' campaign was launched: Kylie went along with it and, although a series of revealing pictures was released towards the end of the year to publicise the LoveKylie swimwear range, on the whole she kept more on than she had done in the past.

Indeed, the tide did seem to be turning. The Chairman of the Professional Association of Teachers, Jim O'Neill, was quoted as saying that Kylie's overtly sexual imagery was beginning to erode the innocence of children: 'Kylie Minogue may be a great singer, but in many of these things you can see more of her bottom than you hear of her voice,' he said. Primary-school girls were going to school in 'ridiculously short skirts', he added, continuing that they were 'dressing like teenagers – it might be appropriate in a club, but certainly not in a school'.

Kylie, ironically, was soon afterwards named as an Ambassador for the National Society of Prevention of Cruelty to Children, in which guise she was to front NSPCC campaigns and act as a children's advocate. 'Cruelty to children is an everyday occurrence which must be stopped,' she said. 'The work undertaken by the NSPCC is essential and I fully support its mission to end child cruelty. I support its vision of a society in which all children are loved and valued. The levels of abuse in this country are shocking. Without charities like the NSPCC they would be worse. Together, we may be able to improve the lives of children within the UK.'

That she takes the work seriously was not in doubt: Kylie had also been involved with the Australian charity Kids Help Line since 1998.

But the remarks, the need for a new image and Olivier's quiet behind-the-scenes influence continued to have an effect on her. As autumn advanced and Kylie began to get ready to publicise her new album *Body Language* and the single from it, 'Slow', she publicly announced that from then on she was staying covered up. 'I'm a 35-year-old woman,' she said. 'I kept everything covered in my video. It's quite tame compared to music TV nowadays.' And would she object if younger rivals took up the baton and stepped out of their clothes? 'There's always competition and it doesn't worry me,' said Kylie. 'They are free to strip down if they like.'

In response to this, the *Sun* launched a petition begging Kylie to reconsider.

The fans minded not one jot. A buzz was beginning to grow around the new album, especially with the news that Ms

Dynamite had penned one of the songs, 'Secret (Take You Home)'. It was to be Kylie's third album for Parlophone, following the extraordinary success of *Light Years* in 2000 and *Fever* the following year and was thought to be more than the equivalent of both, combining her talent for pop melody with up-to-the minute production techniques. In the event, the reviews were extremely positive: 'While Kylie the phenomenon may be increasingly perturbed by the nation's obsession both with her arse and her love life, Kylie the pop princess proves herself here to be entirely at her ease,' said Q magazine.

In November 2003, the single 'Slow' was released and it went straight in at UK No 1, her seventh chart topper. It also finally pushed her ahead of Madonna as the UK's most successful female act of all time: Kylie then had the longest span of number-one singles of any woman, starting with 'I Should Be So Lucky' some 15 years and seven months earlier. Madonna was in second place, with a career of 15 years and one month. Kylie had done it: she was more successful than the Queen of Pop herself, the very woman who had once worn Kylie's name on the most widely viewed billboard in the world.

If she had ever had anything to prove, surely Kylie had done it now: she'd been at the top of one of the world's most fickle professions, survived a brief period out of favour, earned quite a large fortune and had forced the world that once saw her only as Charlene-out-of-*Neighbours* to take her seriously. But Kylie was not one to rest on her laurels. She might have decided not to tour to support *Body Language*, but she was now set to become busier than ever.

Shortly after Kylie's official coronation as the new Queen of Pop, she previewed some of the new tracks at a free concert called Money Can't Buy. *Body Language* went on to perform respectably enough, although it didn't quite manage the same outstanding success as *Fever*. Indeed, some commentators felt it harked back to Kylie's indie days, which were, of course, her professional nadir.

The launch was marked by something else, too: a rare attack on Kylie from one of her colleagues in the music business, Louis Walsh. Perhaps forgetting that she had by this time chalked up 16 years in the business, Walsh, the manager of Westlife, held forth: 'There has to be better talent than Kylie Minogue,' he said. 'She's the most overrated, talentless little girl in the world, apart from Britney Spears. Kylie's not a singer, she's manufactured. She looks good and works the room but there's no real talent there. Kylie and Britney will be forgotten in about five years – they'll be the Debbie Gibson and Tiffany of our time.'

Kylie was unmoved by his words and she could well afford to be. The new album might not have been in quite the same league as the previous two, but that didn't stop the industry lauding her at every turn. America's Grammy Award nominations were announced: Kylie's 'Come Into My World' was there in the Best Dance Category. At the same time, she was nominated in the French NRJ Music Awards both for Best International Female and www.kylie.com went up for Best Musical Website.

And her personal life was on form, too. On Christmas Eve, Kylie and Olivier jetted into Melbourne to spend Christmas with her parents, Dannii and Brendan. For the moment, at least, the relationship appeared to be on track. 'When I met Olivier, suddenly, my life took a wonderful new turn,' Kylie said. 'Olivier makes me content. I know there is an unstoppable interest in my affairs of the heart, but all people need to know is I am very happy.'

She was very successful too, even more than she'd ever been. As Kylie herself freely admits, she has frequently been written off as a lightweight who wouldn't last, but each time she has proven the critics wrong and continues to do so. Kylie was indisputably one of the most famous and successful women in the world by this stage, capable of evolving and more than capable of staying at the very forefront of her career. And, in the coming year, that success was to grow even greater.

Kylie released 'Red Blooded Woman' in 2004 and as part of the promotion did a late-night slot at London's G-A-Y club. Olivier was there and so were 2,000 fans, desperate for a glimpse of their heroine. And the subject on everyone's lips? What Kylie was going to wear. There had been so much talk about covering up and image changes that there was an undercurrent of anxiety in the air. Would Kylie give up the glamour?

And then the lady herself appeared, giving rise to raucous cheers from the audience. The reason was her outfit – a Marlene Dietrich-style ensemble of top hat, split skirt and cane. This was followed up by a display of dancing in which she writhed around before being lifted into the air by male dancers. Kylie might have changed her image – but the raunch factor was still there.

Even so, she presented a more settled appearance than she had done before. Utterly workaholic until she met Olivier, the change in her attitude to her career was still very apparent. 'I usually love work,' she said, 'but I feel different about it now and, yes, that has a lot to do with Olivier. Meeting someone I really want to spend time with and make sacrifices for has made me change. Now, if I had to give up everything tomorrow and go to live in Paris with Olivier, it wouldn't be too terrible. Not too terrible! He is very lovely. He is worldly and wise and there is much to admire about him. He fascinates me in lots of ways. He is dependable – and yet he surprises me often, too.' But, as if to contradict herself, she added, 'Work is part of my life: if I can't go to work and perform, what would I do? Giving up is not that simple. And Olivier would be the last person to encourage that.' With that, she went on to earn £250,000 for a performance at the wedding of the Indian steel magnate Lakshmi Mittal's daughter Vanisha.

Indeed, that performance, although a private one, made quite a splash around the world. So, in fact, did the wedding, one of the most lavish and expensive the world has ever seen and estimated to have cost in total more than £30 million. The five-day extravaganza, celebrating the nuptials of Vanisha to Amit Bhatia, took place in Paris. Kylie's performance took place at a mock castle built just outside the capital, in which she performed on stage for half-an-hour in front of a thousand guests. Her appearance, clad in a short black dress, was a sensation: she started by singing off stage before coming on for the show.

One guest, Amit Rai, was, like everyone else, overawed. 'I pinched myself when Kylie, singing at a private function for the first time, sang "Slow",' he said. 'People didn't have dessert as her performance was more tempting.'

It was Kylie's first ever appearance at such an event, and it garnered almost as much interest as one of her tours.

Kylie was clearly not planning on hanging up her dancing shoes just yet, but speculation really was beginning to mount as to just how she saw her future. In May 2004, Kylie celebrated her 36th birthday, and, while that's no longer considered to be a great age, it is certainly a time when women take stock of whether they really want to have children. And Kylie, for all the talk of cutting her punishing work schedule, showed little sign of wanting to settle down; rather, with another single, 'Chocolate', following hard on the heels of the last, she seemed to be working as hard as ever.

Indeed, the video for 'Chocolate' saw her adopting yet another guise: that of ballet dancer. That new Gallic chic style was more in evidence than ever: this time round we saw Kylie being coached by the choreographer Michael Rooney, working for four days until she got her steps absolutely right for a 40-second ballet routine. 'I nearly killed myself in rehearsals,' she said. 'But the outcome is classy, I hope. It's a lot different from any other videos I've done before. I really wanted to do some ballet in my next video and luckily I've been able to. I normally have three or four hours to practise the choreography for my clips, but this time I had four days to get it right.'

She looked absolutely the part, suggesting that Olivier had been having more influence on her than any of her partners since Michael Hutchence.

Even so, rumours of problems in the relationship with Olivier would not go away. Although the two were spotted on holiday together on the luxury schooner LeLantina, off the coast of Corsica, they still spent long periods apart as Olivier pursued his own film career. Nor was that all. In the summer of 2004, when Kylie went to Australia to launch her latest lingerie range, Olivier was pictured at a party held by P Diddy in St Tropez, getting distinctly personal with the actress Michelle Rodriguez, with whom he'd starred in S.W.A.T. That was not the only time they were seen together: the two were confronted by photographers as they drove through the French seaside resort, and were spotted together giggling in the street.

It all began to look depressingly similar to the James Gooding scenario. At first, a spokesperson for Kylie denied that anything was afoot, but soon after the lady herself appeared in St Tropez to find out what was going on. What was initially billed as a break for the two of them rapidly turned nasty: at lunch in the very fashionable Hotel de La Ponche, their conversation erupted into a row with Kylie walking out. She then left St Tropez while Olivier very pointedly stayed on for another two days. The signs were not looking good.

But then, as so often had happened with James Gooding, there was a reconciliation. Olivier finally followed Kylie back to London, where they were pictured together smiling and looking happy. Some observers believed that Kylie had promised to cut back on work commitments to keep her boyfriend happy, but this was not borne out by Kylie's comments at the time. There had been some completely erroneous speculation earlier in the year that she was pregnant: now Kylie seemed to be implying that that would never happen. 'I know it is a biological matter,' she said. 'When I was younger I didn't know anything about my life, except I thought I'd have kids. Now I'm a bit older, I realise I might not, for one reason or another.'

That reason continued to be her career, which, incidentally, she gave no signs of putting on hold, no matter what Olivier may or may not have said. Amid rumours that she had been spotted talking to Hollywood moguls in Los Angeles and had auditioned for a part in the film *Nanny And The Professor*, Kylie launched details of her next tour, the greatest-hits Kylie – Showgirl tour, to kick off in spring 2005. If any further proof of her continuing popularity were needed, this was it: tickets for the UK leg of the tour sold out within a couple of hours. A London telephone exchange even crashed, such was the demand.

Kylie herself was clearly pleased to be back on the road again. 'I'm so excited to be touring again,' she said. 'It really is the most amazing, challenging and rewarding part of my career and to have the greatest hits and to celebrate is going to be so much fun. This will be the culmination of everything I've done so far, with quite a few surprises. I especially enjoy the period with "Shocked", "What Do I Have To Do" and "Better The Devil You Know", so there may be something from there.'

Clearly, she had missed touring more than she thought.

With the knowledge that *Body Language* had not done that well, Kylie, ever the pragmatist, was clearly prepared to do everything necessary to forestall another career blip. Albums do tend to do better with tours to support them and autumn saw the launch of her greatest-hits album, *Ultimate Kylie*, for which everyone involved had very high hopes. There were no real concerns about the direction she was moving, in, however: by that time, she had sold 20 million singles worldwide and a further 20 million albums. Her record bosses were not worried. 'I Believe In You', co-written by Kylie, Jake Shears and Babydaddy from the Scissor Sisters, was the first single issued to promote the greatest-hits album.

'We were really collaborating and it went really well and I'm happy because I think she had a really good time,' said Jake. 'I think we made some really good stuff. We just got down to business. We were down there for long days so I feel like we got to know each other quite a bit, which was pretty fun.'

And so the pattern that seems to have grown in Kylie's life continued. Her career could not have been more successful, but it took practically no time for rumours to surface of further problems with Olivier. After that short sojourn with

Kylie in London to patch things up, he jetted off to Los Angeles by himself, where he was to stay for the next two months, leaving speculation to grow ever more frenzied about the true state of affairs within the relationship.

Finally, matters got so bad that Kylie herself announced on Australian radio that nothing was wrong. 'We are happy and we are together,' she said. 'I've never really talked about him or about us and I think that has been helpful. There has been endless speculation, stories and rumours, ever since we started seeing each other. It is true that Olivier has been working away in LA and I miss him so much. There isn't any pretending – we have been apart a lot lately.'

To support that, there was also a rather charming story about Olivier then doing the rounds. It was said that, while he was lunching at Chateau Marmont in Hollywood, a girl came over and dangled her room keys in front of him. 'You are beautiful,' said the suave Olivier, 'but I have my woman.'

Kyle's world tour, meanwhile, was being extended amid anxious rumours, quickly dispelled, that she wouldn't be touring Australia, which actually caused quite a fuss in that country, given that it was Kylie's homeland. It was hastily made clear that that was not the case. 'I had someone ask me why I wasn't touring Australia,' said Kylie, 'and I said, "What does your logic tell you? Do you think I'd do that? Of course I'm coming."'

Australia was preparing to honour its famous daughter. The Performing Arts Museum in Melbourne announced plans to hold an exhibition of over 300 of Kylie's most famous costumes from January 2005, with plans to tour the exhibition both throughout Australia and internationally. 'There's everything from Charlene's overalls from *Neighbours* to the gold hotpants from the "Spinning Around" video and the white dress from the "Can't Get You Out Of My Head" video,' said Kylie. 'I'm so happy that my costumes have found a home here in Melbourne, my home town, where I know they will be cared for and preserved. It's such an honour that the Performing Arts Collection wanted it all.'

As the year wore on, the Kylie machine went into full throttle. A huge round of promotional appearances for the new single and album began, alongside work for charity, when the BBC announced that Kylie would appear on the Children In Need appeal on 19 November, where she would perform 'Step Back In Time' and 'Spinning Around'. She also announced plans to perform at 2005's Glastonbury festival. 'She's nervous,' said a friend of Kylie's, adding that she was also very pleased to have been invited. 'She wants to wow the crowds like on her tours. A lot of people will be pleasantly surprised when they see her live.'

Indeed, Kylie had by now made it from the ranks of cheesy teen pop to the supercool. She was now an internationally acclaimed star, with the added status of national treasure in her adopted home of Britain. She also, unusually if not uniquely, had managed to create an image in which she was seen both as a world-class sex symbol and a very nice girl. For all the undulating on camera, deep at heart the nation suspected that Kylie was really a homebody, an impression that was reinforced when she gave an interview is which she confessed to the pleasure she got from dusting.

Kylie was also beginning to experiment with extending her repertoire. She knew it was not only her look that had to evolve, but also her output, and so she began trying out some jazz numbers. She performed a couple of them at a party for the Chloe fashion label in Paris, including the number 'Peel Me A Grape', as well as trying them out in the studio. 'I've done some different jazz and cabaret recordings, which I know sounds terrible when you say it,' confessed Kylie. 'But I enjoyed it and it is the most unlikely thing for me to do, but, when I did it, it was received really well. And because it's so unlikely, it worked.'

In early 2005, the Showgirl tour was launched to great acclaim. The costumes looked like something out of the Moulin Rouge, while all the energy and excitement that had accompanied Kylie's previous tours was out in force. And then, in May, just short of her 37th birthday, Kylie was forced to make an announcement that caused worldwide shock. Kylie Minogue, the very embodiment of youth, femininity and beauty, had found a lump in her breast. After going to the doctor, she was told the worst. It was cancer and the treatment was going to take at least a year.

Initially, Kylie was as professional and dignified about it as could be. She put out a statement through her Australian tour promoters, The Frontier Touring Company, saying that she was going to have to postpone the Australian leg of the tour, and, typically, the emphasis was on worrying about letting her fans down rather than worrying about what was going to happen to her. 'I was so looking forward to bringing the Showgirl tour to Australian audiences,' she said. 'I am sorry to have disappointed my fans. Nevertheless, hopefully all will work out fine and I'll be back with you all again soon.'

Kylie's real state of mind did not become public until much later, but it finally emerged, unsurprisingly, that she had gone into a state of shock. Nor did the massive publicity surrounding the initial announcement help. 'I had one day's grace when I knew and then the next day we made the announcement and then I was virtually a prisoner in the house,' she later confessed.

'Not that I intended to go anywhere but from then on I was just completely thrown into another world. It's really hard for me to express how I felt or even the chain of events. It's such a personal journey. I felt really bad for everyone around me. I'm like, Oh my God, my poor parents. It's like a bomb's dropped. It's still sinking in. It's a very steep learning curve. I would just quietly go to my bedroom and just have 20 minutes to myself and try to deal with everything.'

There was initial speculation and hope among the public that it might not be as bad as all that, but these hopes were dashed extremely quickly, when it turned out Kylie was going to undergo immediate surgery. She was based in Melbourne where her parents were looking after her when it all took place: just nine days before her birthday, a tumour was removed. Olivier was also present; indeed, from that moment onwards he was to provide complete and unconditional love and support to his girlfriend, putting aside once and for all any speculation about the relationship which has proved to be rock solid since then.

'He has been fantastic and has really come through for Kylie,' said a friend of the Minogues. 'She hasn't had much luck with men in the past but Olivier is great for her and the family adore him. He held her hand throughout the tests and was there when she came round after the operation. We know he'll continue to be there for her throughout her recovery.' They were right.

The only person to say anything publicly at this early stage was Dr Jenny Senior, who said that the operation at St Francis Xavier Cabrini Hospital had been a success. 'I feel confident that we caught the cancer in time and that she is now on the road to complete recovery,' she said.

'Kylie has been the perfect patient and has charmed all

my staff. I just wish I could have met her under happier circumstances. Kylie is resting after the operation and her spirits are high and she is feeling fine.'

Dr Senior went on to thank Kylie, her family and Olivier for 'making my job very easy. They were so welcoming. Her spirits are high and she's feeling fine. Kylie has asked me to pass on her thanks once again to all who have expressed their love and concern for her. Your support has certainly helped her through a tough time.'

The Minogue family were also giving their full support. As Kylie began the process of recuperation, everyone gathered round to protect the fragile star, with the siblings telling the world what she had been going through. 'We have all been to see her at hospital and she is going from strength to strength,' said her brother Brendan, now 35 and a cameraman for Australia's Channel 9. 'She is dealing with it all with amazing style and grace. For all the campaigning she has done about cancer awareness, it still doesn't prepare you for that moment when you discover a lump under your skin the size of a golf ball that shouldn't be there. She has had to adapt pretty quickly to all this.

'Dad had prostate cancer and was cured. Kylie has gone to the same hospital as Dad and feels good about that. It is bringing her immense comfort and she just isn't fazed by any of it. We were all so worried about her but Kylie genuinely isn't. She has shown remarkable bravery. I'm so proud of her. No one likes to find a lump beneath their skin and, when she was told it was cancerous, we all kind of went into shock. But she is in good hands. She found the lump in her breast while she was washing and decided to do something about it immediately. When people realise this, I'm sure there will be millions of girls spending a little longer in the shower from now on.'

He was absolutely right: worldwide shock at Kylie's announcement did indeed have people self-examining and contributing to cancer charities, too. Meanwhile, the massive outpourings of affection continued: Kylie had never been as popular as she was now and the world wanted to show her it cared. But still, it seemed, no one had realised quite how serious it had been. Kylie had had the initial surgery, but there was still a great deal more treatment, including chemotherapy, to undergo.

And the shock surrounding her condition seemed to heighten, rather than subside. Perhaps because Kylie has always seemed so fresh and youthful it seemed astounding that she had developed cancer. But it also brought her determination into play. Kylie had now been at the top of the show-business tree for the best part of two decades, not a feat that can be achieved without having a certain amount of inner strength. And so, Kylie turned all the forcefulness she had previously applied to her career into beating this cancer. She was determined she would recover from her illness – but she still had a very long way to go.

17

Kylie's Year Off

Kylie Minogue had been constantly in the limelight since she was in her late teens. She had turned from soap star to warbler to sex symbol to international icon during that time, constantly reinventing herself, and becoming one of the best-loved stars in the world in the process. For years now, every move Kylie made had been watched, analysed and reported on, and, while at times it must have been irksome, it also kept Kylie in the limelight and ahead in her career. Now, for the first time in decades, she really wanted to be left alone.

And so, to a certain extent, she was, but, even so, the papers could not resist snatched pictures of her when she presented a very different face to the world from the one the public was accustomed to seeing. She was pictured looking gaunt and ill shortly after the operation, as she was escorted to a car by a protective Olivier, and the sunglasses and hat she wore did nothing to disguise how frail she had become. The world was alarmed.

Support continued to pour in from all over the world, with Prince Charles, no less, sending her a note wishing her a speedy recovery, alongside Sir Elton John and Robbie Williams. And, as her programme of radiotherapy began, Kylie moved out of the parental home, simply to escape the gaggle of reporters that were outside waiting for her every day.

'Kylie is finally getting the peace and privacy she needs to recover,' said a source close to the singer. 'But there is still a long, long way to go and more time to recover.'

Another wave of moral support came from the Glastonbury Festival. Kylie had been due to perform there before having to call off her tour and, during the Saturday headline set by Coldplay, singer Chris Martin paid tribute to the absent star to massive cheers from the audience, saying, 'Everyone's paid to see Kylie as well, so shouldn't we salute absent friends?'

The band then charged into a note-perfect cover of 'Can't Get You Out Of My Head' and got the biggest response from the crowd of the evening.

Kylie was extremely touched and posted a notice on her website. 'I was deeply moved to hear about the tributes at Glastonbury,' it read. 'Though I'm desperately sad not to have been able to perform at the event, I was so happy to feel that I was, in a small way, still a part of it. My humble thanks to the artists and the crowd. I'm far away but I hope you felt the smile on my face and the joy it brought me. Hope a great time was had by all. Love Kylie.'

But there was a hint of cheer shortly afterwards when Kylie released a statement saying that the chemotherapy had been a success. Dannii made an appearance at the *Vanity Fair* party to launch the Diamonds exhibition at London's Natural History Museum, where she, too was upbeat: 'Isn't the news just great?' she asked. 'She's been inspirational, she's a fighter. I want to be there to support her and we both give huge thanks to the well-wishers.'

Kylie's positive attitude was certainly coming through loud and clear. Putting paid to rumours that she had moved to Europe to escape the press, she turned up at the Royal Children's Hospital in Melbourne, where she met children who had been struck by the disease. She didn't actually say anything about her own condition, but clearly provided a boost for the young patients. 'There's a champ, there's a champ coming by,' said one.

Kylie's concern about children was not a one-off. Despite the fact that she was very far from being in the best of health, she took some time to help persuade UK immigration authorities to grant visas to Sri Lankan child actors who were left as orphans after the tsunami tragedy to perform *Children of the Sea* by Toby Gough. A letter she wrote to the British High Commission was used to support their case and Gough was overwhelmed.

'I couldn't believe it when I got a reply giving her support for the whole project to be brought to the Edinburgh Festival,' he said. 'I sent it to the British High Commission which was considering the visa applications along with other supporting letters and I am sure it helped swing things our way. Then, when she agreed to actually help us to meet the cost of taking the kids to Edinburgh, that was wonderful. The play is all about human survival so perhaps that struck a chord with what she is going through. When you think what she has on her mind at the moment, it is absolutely fantastic that she has taken the time to organise some support for us. The children have all written to her to say thank you.'

She was helping people indirectly, too. In August, it was reported that, as a result of 'The Kylie Effect', screenings for breast cancer had risen by as much as 40 per cent. 'It's encouraging to hear that Kylie's unfortunate diagnosis has led to more Australian women realising the importance of early detection and attending screening appointments,' said Dr Sarah Rawlings, head of policy at UK charity Breakthrough Breast Cancer.

'Breakthrough has witnessed thousands more web hits and calls since this news broke. In the UK, all women are entitled to screening from the age of 50 and we encourage these women to attend their appointments. Women should also get to know how their breasts look and feel normally so they can see their GP if they notice any changes – early detection is vital for prompt treatment and improving the chances of survival.'

Aware that her treatment was going to continue for months to come, Kylie made the decision to move to Paris to be with Olivier. She was pictured for the very first time wearing a headscarf. It took some courage to appear in public as she did: Kylie, after all, was known as an international beauty and style icon and to be pictured coping with the side-effects of the treatment took some guts.

This was backed up by Dannii, who, with Kylie unavailable for comment, was rapidly becoming a sort of pseudo-spokeswoman for her sister. She was coping 'gracefully', said Dannii, and had found worldwide messages of goodwill 'very helpful and supportive. Sis is doing really good. It's quite a stressful treatment. Anyone who is going through that would know that it is physical and mental. She is handling it very gracefully and I would just have to say that, honouring her privacy, I wouldn't want to go into any details of anything. It's a tough time on the family as well. But she wishes anyone else going through this, she wishes them all of her love and all the best as well.'

And Kylie continued to try to use her celebrity to boost

awareness of the cause, as the following message from her website shows:

> This October is Breast Cancer Awareness Month so it's time to 'Think Pink!' It's about raising awareness and helping raise funds for research and support. This is absolutely essential in the fight against breast cancer and the cure we all hope to find. You can find a lot of information at these official sites: www.breakthrough.org.uk,
> www.breastcancercare.org.uk and
> www.cancervic.org.au.
>
> As for me, I would love to be at some of the wonderful benefits taking place, but my doctors have advised against it at this stage of my treatment. I wish all of the fundraising activities well (wonder how many shaved heads there will be this year?!) and hope that fun is had whilst promoting such an important issue. I send my solidarity to those whose lives have been affected by breast cancer and my thanks to those who are helping in each and every way.
>
> Love Kylie X

This was a message that was repeated at the Pink Ice Ball at The Dorchester hotel. Kylie was too ill to attend herself, but again sent a message of support to everyone who was there. 'I'm sorry I can't be with you this evening,' she wrote. 'I'm currently a cancer patient. I aim to be a cancer survivor. This is only possible with the incredible work done by so many in the field – doctors, specialists, scientists and volunteers. I have been on a crash course of learning in the last few months and now have first-hand experience of how vital awareness, funding and support is.

'I send my solidarity to those whose lives have been affected by breast cancer and my thanks to those who are helping in each and every way. Enjoy your evening and hope to see you soon. Love Kylie.'

And so it went on. The press, while constantly fascinated by what was going on with the world's favourite pop star, actually treated Kylie with a great deal of respect. She was pictured from time to time, always wearing a headscarf, unfailingly polite and charming, no matter how rotten she felt. Sometimes she was up to going out and shopping; at other times, she stayed at home, being cared for by Olivier and her family. There was the odd weekend away with Olivier, too, although everything was conducted on a quiet scale.

There was a good deal of speculation, too, about the state of Kylie's health, but what rumblings did emerge from the Minogue camp did on the whole appear positive. Kylie was put on a special diet to help her gain weight: she went up to six-and-a-half stone, the heaviest she has ever been. Public affection, and great respect for the way she was handling herself, continued to soar. There was a sense of real celebration when she was strong enough to return to her parents in Australia for a visit, to say nothing of hopes that Kylie was on the mend.

And, indeed, she was. The news came out, in a very low-key way, that she was getting much better. And then Kylie began appearing without her headscarf, showing off a sleek new look, as her hair had clearly begun to grow back. Finally, what really convinced everyone that she really was much better was when, shortly after her 38th birthday, she joined Dannii on stage as the latter performed at London's G-A-Y club, thrilling the crowd.

'It was amazing,' said Dannii of the song they sang together, 'Jump To The Beat'. 'You know, I see her all the time. But it's good for the fans to see that she's well, she's healthy and she's back on stage. I knew Kylie was going to be at the club to watch me perform because we'd spoken on the phone earlier – but I didn't know she was going to go on stage. She asked me what the set list was and when I said I was doing some of the old songs she said she wanted to come. I was thinking to myself, It's going to be a nightmare getting her in and hiding her at the club. And I warned her it would be really hot.

'I'd come off before the last song and I saw her standing at the side of the stage. I assumed she would do a runner just while I was doing the last number so she could get out without being mobbed. I had my earplugs on so I couldn't hear what people were saying around me. Then she came out on stage, which was a real surprise. For me it was about having my big sister there supporting me. She came on and was being like an older sister. She came on and said, "I have a bone to pick with you."

'And I said, "What?"

'She said, "You have to sing 'Jump To The Beat'."

'The pictures were so cute and I was thinking about how my grandma in Australia would love it when she saw them. It was the next day that I realised what it meant to all the fans. There was a real triumphant mood to it after the last year, seeing her standing there glowing, beaming and, of course, with a microphone in her hand. For all those Australian fans who have been holding on to tickets for the tour she had to cancel, it would have been a good signal that she will be back soon.'

But it was not just a lift for her fans; her family was delighted, too. 'Last year was a hard one,' said Dannii. 'I think every family goes through a hard year. No one lives in a perfect world. You get hit by things that surprise you. But I'm just grateful that this is now a happy year for us. I get fed up talking about bad times. Now it's a happy time, she is better and the nightmare is over. So let's all accept that it's over and let's all rejoice that she is better. I think it's made every woman more conscious about breast cancer but I really don't want to become a spokeswoman for breast cancer awareness. I just wanted to be a good sister and I'm only just coming out of that mode of protecting, caring, supporting and being there. I had to get my head around it all too, but the most important thing is that everyone stops talking about it. I know other people who have had cancer in their families and after a while they just don't want to talk about it. You don't want to talk about it every second of every day.

'Once it's over, let it go. I like to live in the moment. Now I want to move on.'

So did everyone else – and, at long last, they could.

18

Back in the Spotlight

It was an extraordinary recovery. Kylie Minogue had been out of the limelight for a year and, when the occasional photo appeared, she looked weak and frail. But, by June 2006, it was announced that the chemotherapy had been successful and she had been given the all-clear. Many people might have decided to take it easy for a while after what had, after all, been a gruelling year, but Kylie was having none of it.

For a woman as focused and ambitious as she is, it had been torture being forced to stay at home, waiting helplessly until she was told that she was well enough to venture out once more, and the moment she knew she'd beaten her illness, the formidable Kylie machine swung back into action. Desperately keen to make up for lost time, an album and a tour were both announced at a press conference in Melbourne, held by her tour manager Michael Gudinski. It also emerged that she had written a book while she was ill, *Showgirl Princess*. There was a real sense of happiness in the air as Michael cracked open a bottle of champagne and announced that Kylie was back.

'She's definitely through the worst of everything, she's so determined and she can't wait to see you all,' said Michael. 'Obviously she's still got a few mountains to climb, but we're very confident that the tour will be going ahead in November.

'You can't keep Kylie down. She's actually recording in the studio and working on songs as we speak. She is still getting tired on the odd day, but she looked as fit as a fiddle. We're going to take as much pressure off her as we can.' That was partly to be achieved by lengthening the time on the tour in order to allow Kylie to rest.

She started making appearances in public, too. Kylie had reinvented her look on numerous occasions in the past, and now the old trooper actually used the suffering of the past year to her advantage. Her hair was now growing back, and she had it cut into a 1920s bob, a gamine style that suited her delicate features down to the ground. The smile was more full on than ever as she rediscovered her power as an icon.

It was announced that the Victoria and Albert Museum, no less, would be holding an exhibition of her costumes, from that famous pair of gold hotpants to some of her most spectacular stage displays.

'The V&A regularly puts on exhibitions of fashion, costume, design and contemporary culture,' said a spokeswoman. 'This collection, which launches in February, will look at Kylie's changing image, what goes into the creation of a popular icon and why it's successful.'

Kylie herself had remained largely quiet while all this was going on, working behind the scenes on plans to relaunch herself, until she was sure she was strong enough to step centre stage once more. That moment finally came when she made an appearance at Sir Elton John's annual White Tie and Tiara Ball at the end of June. She looked stunning, wearing a

Chanel dress and Bulgari jewellery worth £3 million, leaving everyone in no doubt that a full recovery was on the cards. 'It's a miracle I got better,' she said to her fellow guests. 'It's my official coming out.'

Fellow guests were awestruck. 'There was a collective intake of breath when Kylie arrived,' said one. 'People were going up to her and telling her how amazing she looked.'

She did indeed. And now back in the spotlight, she decided to give an interview about the impact of the previous year, an interview that served a number of purposes. It cleared up a good deal of the speculation, it showed her in glowing health and it also warned that, although she had been very fortunate in that the cancer had been discovered early, she knew she could take nothing for granted in life.

In the interview with Cat Deeley on Sky One, Kylie recalled the moment her doctor broke the news that something was very badly wrong. 'I went silent,' said Kylie. 'My mum and dad were with me, then we all went to pieces.' Of course, Kylie was due to start the next leg of her tour, and, incredibly, her initial impulse was to go ahead. 'I was saying, "No, I've got my flight to Sydney in two hours. I'm getting on a plane,"' she recalled.

It was her father Ron who made her see sense, saying, 'No. You're not getting a plane. You'll just sit down.'

Kyle sparkled in the interview. Covered in diamonds, she looked more beautiful than ever: the message clearly was: I'm back.

But, even so, her light-hearted demeanour and cheery presence did not conceal the fact that she'd had a very frightening year. 'Having had cancer, one important thing to know is you're still the same person at the end, you are the same person during it,' she said. 'You're stripped down to, you know, you're down near zero. But it seems that most people come out at the other end feeling more like themselves than ever before. I'm more eager than ever to do what I did. I want to do everything. I don't want it to sound soppy but that's the way it is. Try to enjoy the moment. Have a laugh. Swim in the sea. Hug and kiss.'

Kylie was also deeply grateful to her fans, and when she talked about some of the letters she received, from the very young to the very old, it was clear the measure of her popularity is not in doubt.

'We don't want doctors to put needles into you,' wrote one little girl. 'When are you back on stage?'

But Kylie was also aware that, as an immensely popular figure and role model, her so far successful battle with the disease will have given others hope. 'I know there will be people who will see this, be watching this now, there will be X amount of women being diagnosed,' she said. 'I love to say: you can get through it. You can.'

Kylie also revealed for the first time that, even before she found the lump, there were indications that something might be wrong. Very unusually for her, she even began to have doubts about her capability to stage such a colossal tour. 'I distinctly recall going to my two sound guys and saying, "Maybe I'm too old for this? I'm so tired,"' she said, also adding that she had started to come out in cold sweats.

Her self-doubt, as much as anything else, was an indication that something was wrong. Kylie was not too old to be doing what she was doing – Madonna, a decade her senior, is still going strong – and she should have been at the peak of her physical fitness rather than feeling so drained.

After the partial mastectomy operation, Kylie stayed with her family in Melbourne for two months. And, whether or not she was actually aware of it, her determination almost certainly played a key role in her recovery – after all, it is often said that, when it comes to cancer, it is the positive patients who get well. 'Always one to rise to the challenge, I thought, OK, OK, you've got to fight it,' she said. 'You can't sit back and let everyone else do the work for you. Time keeps ticking, you go through the motions. I don't want to go into the doom and gloom of it. It's hard. On days you didn't see me – or no one saw me – were the days that I simply couldn't get up or could not do anything. To walk to the corner store was a great... I did it. I got to the cafe. And then I'd go home.'

Despite the fact that the world had seen the pictures of her looking so frail, Kylie's words still came as a shock. Over and over it became apparent quite how serious this illness had been. And her positivity and determination came up trumps, not least when, still in the early days, she decided to visit a children's cancer ward. 'That day the father of an ill child eyeballed me and said, "And how are you doing?"' she recalled. 'I said, "Fine, fine," and managed to go off and find a corner to contain myself.'

In fact, there was still a lengthy course of chemotherapy to undergo, and Kylie was faced with a difficult choice. While her family had been looking after her in Australia, Olivier had to return to France. Should she stay at home or travel with him? The relationship had been growing increasingly strong during the previous months, on top of which there were some of the world's greatest experts when it came to cancer in Paris. And so Kylie decided that she would accompany him to France, where she would have treatment at the Gustave-Roussy Institute, one of Europe's leading centres of cancer treatment, therapy and research.

'My parents did not want me to leave Australia, but I had to have some semblance of what my life is,' she said. 'I've a life with my boyfriend in Paris and I was quite determined I was going to it there. Of course, my mum came with me.'

It is a measure of her strength of mind that Kylie was not only able to cope with what happened next, but she was able to talk about it, too. Being in her late thirties and about to undergo a course of chemotherapy, she was told that it was almost certain there would be an effect on her fertility. For a woman who wanted to have children, this was a serious blow.

'I've just rolled along,' said Kylie, when she was asked if she'd made a conscious decision to postpone motherhood. 'The past few years have been pretty full on. I didn't have much time to stop and think about it... I love children – always have, always will.'

In the light of that, Kylie decided to undergo a procedure which, if truth be told, has only extremely limited chances of success. Tiny segments of her ovaries were removed and frozen, in the hope that they will one day make it possible for her to have her own biological children. However, this course of action has only ever worked twice before. Kylie remained determinedly upbeat. 'I would love them,' she said. 'We'll have to see.'

Another issue that Kylie had to deal with was losing her hair, a traumatic occurrence for any woman, but especially one who has been such a famed beauty as Kylie. Again, she took it on the chin, merely saying that she became extremely competent at tying a headscarf. 'It wasn't so much of an issue for me,' she said. 'I'm used to having different looks. There was a price on my head at that time: who's going to get a picture of her with a bus flying by and my scarf coming off? I don't want to be like, I had this, this, this. That's boring, it's personal and I don't want to remind people of that. This is coming out the other side. It's like springtime.'

Dannii helped, too. 'She would come to Paris on the Eurostar, put the music on, get me moving.'

Of course, even Kylie had her very dark days. 'That was a very difficult time, waiting for the phone to ring or for the doctor to come over,' she said of the period when she had to wait to see if the chemo had worked. 'I can hardly believe that I'm here.'

Nor was that the end of it. Although the chemotherapy had been successful, Kylie now had to undergo a course of radiation to try to ensure that the cancer did not come back. She did, however, begin to see a physical recovery; initially, she had shaved her hair off in one go so that she wouldn't have to see it falling out bit by bit, and now it was finally beginning to grow back again. 'When it starts to grow back it's so thrilling,' she said. 'There's an eyelash! There's an eyebrow! You are sure you'll be the one for whom it never does.'

Although she was out of danger, Kylie was both aware of the effort it would take to go back on stage again, and the fact that it was still possible the cancer might return.

'I've got a mountain to climb, but I don't fancy hanging around the bottom of the mountain,' she said. 'I'm not sure I'll be able to do everything I did before. No more quick changes. We'll have slow changes and maybe even a little chair backstage. I'm not like this all the time. It's no picnic and I'm still going through it. It's not like, Hey, it's over. I still have medical treatments. I still have check-ups. I'm aware and I do all the things I'm supposed to do to stay on top of things. Had I not discovered the cancer until a little later, the story might have been very different. I was saved, I really was.'

Very tellingly, the moment in the interview in which Kylie is finally moved to tears is the thought that the cancer might have put paid to her professional career forever.

But it hadn't. The warmth with which Kylie was welcomed back was phenomenal. When dates were announced for her resumed Showgirl tour, tickets sold out for the London dates in six minutes and the organisers had to arrange a further two shows.

Kylie posted a message on her website. 'I wanted to let you all know that I am totally overwhelmed by the ticket sales today for my Wembley shows in January,' it read. 'Thank you all so much for your loyalty and make sure and have your dancing shoes ready for the concerts, love to you all Kylie. X'

'The demand for Kylie is absolutely phenomenal and these are the fastest-selling shows I have ever experienced,' said her spokesman Dave Chumbley. 'It will be fantastic to see her back on stage again.'

The Sky interview had also gone down extremely well. Kylie's frankness about her illness and how it had affected her had touched a good many hearts, be they existing fans, fellow cancer sufferers or merely people who felt sympathy for what she had been through. It had been draining to do, but there was an indication of the fact that Kylie was returning to her old self.

'After I interviewed Kylie about her breast cancer ordeal, I thought she would be feeling emotionally drained and wanting to go straight home,' said Cat. 'In fact, she said to me, "OK, let's go home first, Cat." Then she was like, "Oh, get changed, because we are going out to dinner and I am determined to wear my diamonds."

'So the pair of us got dolled up to the nines, put on our best sparklers and went to Mr Chow's Chinese restaurant in Knightsbridge. It was great because the paparazzi did not see us coming to such a local restaurant and we weren't disturbed.

'I'm glad because I think Kylie really desperately needed that little bit of peace and quiet. So, there we were, just two girls, ridiculously overdressed, and we just could not stop laughing. We ate loads and talked about really normal things like the weather and fashion. I'd say it was the very moment Kylie got back her sparkle.'

And, as Kylie's appearances in public became more frequent, so she seemed to exult in being able to go out and live it up once more. Appearing at the premiere of *Brasil Brasileiro* in London at the Sadler's Wells Theatre, she couldn't resist a quick twirl to the music herself. It cheered her up as well as everyone present, while sending out a definite message: I'm back.

And, once she'd got started, it seemed impossible to calm her down. Her next appearance, and the first she made on stage since being diagnosed with cancer, was at the Edinburgh Festival. It was at a performance of *Havana Rumba!* on the Edinburgh Fringe: the show's producer, Toby Gough, pulled her on the stage to join in. Kylie was in town to support *Finding Marina*, a show she helped to finance, which was performed by Sri Lankan children who had lost everything after the dreadful Boxing Day tsunami in 2004.

'I had drunk two bottles of rum on my own,' said Toby the next day. 'It was a wild night. The audience was going crazy. We always ask her to come and see the shows, but we didn't know it was going to be last night.'

They did indeed. Kylie was dressed relatively modestly compared to what she usually wore on stage, namely jeans, a pink and white top and black hat, but she nearly brought the house down. 'It appears no one noticed Kylie in the audience and it was a shock to see her on stage,' said spokesman Andrew Neilson. 'She looked fantastic – it was obvious she enjoyed herself. But she almost did not make it, as the stage manager was not going to let her on at first.'

Indeed, Kylie was looking so fantastic that everyone around her could hardly believe it. Her health certainly looked to have returned and she was simply so happy to be out there again that her happiness was contagious. Kevin Murphy, her hairdresser, was also struck by how vibrant she appeared.

'Kylie's illness has dramatically changed her,' he said. 'It's like she's been reborn – now she loves life. She was tired before. There was always a team of people around her. She's actually separated herself from all that by going to live in France. She's got a few houses here and there, but she's learning to speak French. She can live a normal life there. She doesn't have to live like a pop star. She's lived her entire life in front of the camera and what she enjoys now is simple pleasures. She loves to pop down the shops, whip round a boutique and then have a cup of tea at home.'

Indeed, it was beginning to seem as if the cancer, initially so devastating, had given Kylie a whole new lease of life. It had certainly provided her with the opportunity to sit back and assess her life for the first time in years. Under normal circumstances – or what could be called normal for Kylie – life was always absolutely frenetic and now, despite the difficult circumstances surrounding it, she had been forced to think about how she really wanted to run her life.

'When I saw her a few weeks ago, I was amazed,' said Kevin. 'I said, "This is the best you've looked for eight years." It's like a rebirth. She's been pretty thin in the past but at the moment she's a bit plump. She's getting a lot of pleasure from her food. She's beginning to enjoy red wine too, which she never used to. We'd go out for dinner and I'd end up finishing hers because she would only ever have one glass. But now she's started to drink good, expensive red wine. She's not a lush, she's just likes it. I'm sure it's Olivier and the French influence because they love life. Before the cancer, Kylie was a workaholic. When you work all the time, it's hard to maintain your health. Now she's relaxing and the extra weight helps her look younger. Her complexion is a really nice pale pink colour, like peaches and cream.'

Kevin was certainly in a good position to tell. He and Kylie had been working together for years, both home and on tours, as he explained when talking about her magnificent wigs. 'You just stick them on, it's much easier when she goes on stage,' he said. 'She has fine, delicate hair. It's dry because it's got colour in it. Her natural colour is dark blonde. She likes to be strawberry blonde.

'When I last saw her, her hair had just grown back after the chemotherapy. It has given her a new look. I told her not to grow it long. It looks fantastic short; it really suits her. It's the best she's looked in years. It's just so fresh, it makes her look more petite. Long hair was dragging her down a little. Now she looks modern and natural. When I told her I really liked it short, she said, "Maybe I won't grow it then."'

Like some others of her acquaintance, though, including Elle Macpherson, Kevin admitted that he had found Kylie's cancer hard to deal with. 'I'm scared of people who get ill,' he said. 'I tend to run for cover and don't quite know what to say. When I heard, I sent her a little box of really dumb things like hand cream and a gold chain. I didn't really know how to cope, to tell you the truth. I always had this thing in my mind that she was invincible. She's absolutely fine now and I am overjoyed. I'm sure she's still got to be a bit careful but when I saw her she was as right as rain. We talk over email and on the telephone and catch up over a cup of tea when we get the chance.'

Elle, incidentally, also went on record about the fact that she was sorry she hadn't been in touch. 'It is one of my biggest regrets that, when I heard Kylie had been diagnosed with cancer, I didn't pick up the phone and call her right away,' she said. 'I do know her. We've been in the same circles for years. I assumed she'd have family and closer friends around her. You don't want to intrude. I feel so guilty about that now because she could probably have done with as much support as possible. Sometimes we shy away from grief or difficult situations but I've learned a lesson with Kylie.'

Kevin, meanwhile, like so many others, was quick to point out that Kylie's relationship with Olivier was going from strength to strength, pouring scorn on any comments that he might be a bit of a womaniser. 'Olivier is a dream,' he said. 'He stood by her the whole way. If you are a womaniser, you'd be looking for a way out, but he was there all the time. They're always cuddling, laughing and joking around. He's not bothered by fashion, he's a real man. We were talking about hair products and he told me he'd been using something he thought was a face moisturiser for a month – before Kylie pointed out to him that it was for hair!'

Kylie might have been taking a more relaxed attitude to life, but she was still keen to get back to work. And so she started on a programme of rebuilding her physical strength, using cardio and dance routines. 'You know, my energy's coming back now,' she said. 'I am so revved up. I can't wait to get back to my day job.'

Even so, this newly learned ability to relax had not gone away: she was pictured with Olivier having a holiday in the South of France.

Towards the end of July, Kylie's book, *Showgirl Princess*, was launched. Kylie made a personal appearance at Puffin, her publishers, on the Strand in London, at a talk for buyers, the people who put in orders for the books for bookshops. Wayne Winstone from Ottakar's was very impressed. 'She was friendly, charming and down-to-earth,' he said. 'I asked her if she would do signings in Basildon and Croydon. I was trying to think of locations that contrasted with her lifestyle. She said she would be more than happy.'

The book, as its title implied, told the story of a girl called Kylie who, with a little help from her stylists and friends, turns into – you guessed it – a showgirl princess. It was full of pictures by William Baker, and, though it was aimed at children, it was widely expected that adult fans would show some interest, too.

'It's not autobiographical, although Kylie does draw on her experiences,' said a spokesperson for Puffin. 'The book is for little girls who dream of dressing up and going on stage and it's written in a tone that's suitable for children. The main character just happens to be Kylie.'

'It's a wonderful book which will appeal to little princesses everywhere who love to have fun!' said Jane Richardson, senior editor at Puffin, who along with managing director Francesca Dow visited Kylie in Paris.

'I met with the girls from Puffin at the local cafe,' says Kylie 'wearing my headscarf. We spoke about the storyline, and what we wanted to do… and did it! It was something that I had thought about since the tour. I get such cute little notes from kids that I just wanted to do a kids book somehow.'

And it also helped to take her mind of her illness. 'It was something different that wasn't physically challenging which I could do at that time,' she said. 'I couldn't do anything else, but I could – if I felt up to it – sit at my computer and work on the book. A lot of it was done by email. The illustrator was in New York and she would send me her ideas and then I would send her back my thoughts and then we would add other images and polish it until it was perfect.'

This was some work ethic – even if Kylie couldn't get out there physically as she had done before, she still managed to find a project to keep her mind off what she was going through.

Kylie had also become very attached to Sheba, Olivier's puppy – and vice versa. 'Oh, don't get me started on Sheba,' she said. 'When I met Olivier in Los Angeles, he was with Sheba. At first, she was a little resistant to the idea of there being another woman in Olivier's life. There was an incident when she took a shoe from my wardrobe and chewed it to bits, but it was just a territorial thing – the kind of thing that happens when there are two women in a man's life. Now she's based in Paris and we are devoted to each other. She even came to the Chanel show with me earlier this year. She was very important during my treatment – there were many long hugs during that time.'

Indeed, as well as being a time of reflection, Kylie's illness had brought her closest relationship into sharp focus. Although she had always had a very strong relationship with both parents, this, if anything, strengthened the bond still further. 'My relationship with my parents has always been close,' she said. 'My mother, in particular, has always been more like a friend to me. But, when I was diagnosed, it was like they needed to be my mother and father again, not my friends. It was as if I was a little girl to them again. I was so lucky to have my mum with me in Paris throughout my treatment. I don't know how I would have got through that without her.'

By this time, Kylie was back in full swing. She launched a 2007 diary, full of quite stunning pictures of her, and was now regularly seen in a series of ever more extravagant evening gowns to show off her healthy appearance. Her popularity, if anything, had soared still further in the time she was away, and, as if to emphasise this, she was named as one of the top 15 most influential pop stars of the last 25 years, in a poll to mark music channel MTV's own 25th anniversary.

Bono came very top of the list, followed by Michael Jackson and Madonna, while the other stars named were Kurt Cobain, Prince, Eminem, Kylie Minogue, Snoop Dogg, Justin Timberlake, Sir Elton John, Beyonce Knowles, Robbie Williams, Pete Doherty, Christina Aguilera and Britney Spears.

She was now also ready to talk about the new album, on which she had teamed up with the Scissor Sisters. 'When I went back into the studio, I was very nervous, but it was very good to discover that everything was still working,' she said. 'I hadn't sung for more than a year and it was reassuring to know that nothing had changed.'

But something had. Kylie's own level of self-awareness, of what her career meant to her, but also of what her relationships and other aspirations were had changed through a profound period of reflection. Kylie had met one of life's biggest challenges with courage, vivacity and style. Her return to centre stage was greeted with a kind of rapture by her fans, and with a goodwill almost unprecedented towards any other figure in show business. Kylie, showgirl extraordinaire, was back.